ADDISON-WESLEY

QUEST 2000

EXPLORING MATHEMATICS

AUTHORS

Ricki Wortzman   Lalie Harcourt   Brendan Kelly   Peggy Morrow

Randall I. Charles   David C. Brummett   Carne S. Barnett

CONTRIBUTING AUTHORS

Linda Beatty   Anne Boyd   Fred Crouse   Susan Gordon

Elisabeth Javor   Alma Ramirez   Freddie Lee Renfro   Mary M. Soniat-Thompson

REVISED EDITION

Addison-Wesley Publishers Limited

Don Mills, Ontario • Reading, Massachusetts • Menlo Park, California
New York • Wokingham, England • Amsterdam • Bonn
Sydney • Singapore • Tokyo • Madrid • San Juan • Paris
Seoul • Milan • Mexico City • Taipei

Reviewers/Consultants

Marie Beckberger, Springfield Public School, Mississauga, Ontario
Jan Carruthers, Somerset and District Elementary School, King's County, Nova Scotia
Garry Garbolinsky, Tanner's Crossing School, Minnedosa, Manitoba
Darlene Hayes, King Edward Community School, Winnipeg, Manitoba
Barbara Hunt, Bayview Hill Elementary School, Richmond Hill, Ontario
Rita Janes, Roman Catholic School Board, St. John's, Newfoundland
Karen McClelland, Oak Ridges Public School, Richmond Hill, Ontario
Betty Morris, Edmonton Catholic School District #7, Edmonton, Alberta
Jeanette Mumford, Early Childhood Multicultural Services, Vancouver, B.C.
Evelyn Sawicki, Calgary Roman Catholic Separate School District #1, Calgary, Alberta
Darlene Shandola, Thomas Kidd Elementary School, Richmond, B.C.
Elizabeth Sloane, Dewson Public School, Toronto, Ontario
Denise White, Morrish Public School, Scarborough, Ontario
Elizabeth Wylie, Clark Boulevard Public School, Brampton, Ontario

Technology Advisors

Fred Crouse, Centreville, Nova Scotia; Flick Douglas, North York, Ontario; Cynthia Dunham, Framingham, MA; Susan Seidman, Toronto, Ontario; Evelyn J. Woldman, Framingham, MA; Diana Nunnaley, Maynard, MA

Editorial Coordination: McClanahan & Company
Editorial Development: Susan Petersiel Berg, Margaret Cameron, Mei Lin Cheung, Fran Cohen/First Folio Resource Group, Inc., Lynne Gulliver, Louise MacKenzie, Helen Nolan, Mary Reeve

Design: McClanahan & Company
Wycliffe Smith Design

Cover Design: The Pushpin Group

Canadian Cataloguing in Publication Data

Wortzman, Ricki
Quest 2000 : exploring mathematics, grade 5,
revised edition: student book

First and third authors in reverse order on
previous ed.
ISBN 0-201-55272-8

I. Mathematics – Juvenile literature. I. Harcourt,
Lalie, 1951– . II. Kelly, B. (Brendan), 1943–
III. Title.

QA107.K45   1997   510   C95-932756-8

Pearson Education Canada

ISBN 0-201-55272-8

This book contains recycled product and is acid free.

Printed and bound in Canada.

12 13 ITIB 04 03

Table of Contents

Height (cm)	Ideal mass (kg)
152	45
168	58.5
162	54
170	60.75
157	49.5

*H*ow can we use patterns to predict?

Time of Day	Temperature
10 a.m.	20°
12 p.m.	24°
7 a.m.	18°
3 p.m.	27°

**DISCOVERING PATTERNS
AND RELATIONSHIPS**

S·T·A·R·T·I·N·G
OUT

**Look for a pattern
in these dancers' arms.**

1 • Describe the patterns you see here.

• How are the patterns alike? How are they different?

• Where have you seen other patterns like these?
Describe them.

Look for a pattern on each shirt.

Look for a pattern on the baseball.

My Journal: What types of patterns do you find interesting?

S·T·A·R·T·I·N·G OUT

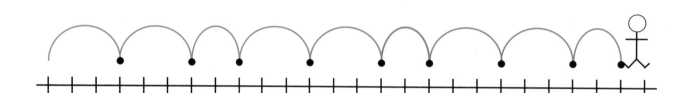

2 • Describe a pattern you see here.

• Draw a number line like the one above. Write some numbers along the line. Talk about the pattern you have created.

• How are the two patterns you described alike? How are they different?

3 Kevin likes babysitting Keisha. He really likes the pattern he sees in this T-table!

Hours worked	Pay
3	$12
4	$16
5	$20
6	$24

- Describe the pattern.

- What other patterns like this can you think of?

My Journal: What makes a pattern?

Growth Patterns and Relationships

▶ How can you describe the pattern that relates the height of the diving platform to the number of tiles needed in all?

Summer Olympics

Height of Diving Platform	Number of Tiles in All
2	5
3	6
4	7
5	?
6	?
7	?
8	?
9	?
10	?

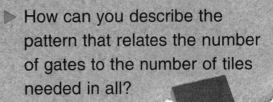

How can you describe the
pattern that relates the number
of gates to the number of tiles
needed in all?

Number of Gates	Number of Tiles in All
1	5
2	10
3	15
4	?
5	?
6	?
7	?

Thebes, Egypt

ON YOUR OWN

1. For each table, write a rule that explains how to find the output number when you know the input number. Copy and complete the table.

a.

Input	Output
2	4
4	8
5	10
7	14
12	24
20	?
50	?

b.

Input	Output
10	3
15	8
20	13
25	18
30	23
35	?
40	?

2. Draw pictures of the next two designs in this tile pattern. Write the rule in words. Copy and complete the table.

Number of Gates	Number of Tiles
1	6
2	12
3	18
4	?
5	?
6	?

3. Make up data for a T-table that follows a rule. Exchange tables with a classmate and find each other's rule.

4. *My Journal:* What have you learned about patterns and tables?

Creating, Analyzing, and Extending Patterns

1. How many boxes should be in the bottom row in a pyramid with 45 boxes?

Number of Boxes in Bottom Row	Total Number of Boxes
1	1
2	3
3	6
4	?
5	?
6	?
7	?

2. A patio was designed like the one below. There are 50 tiles available. How many tiles should be placed in the middle row to use the greatest number of tiles?

Number of Tiles in Middle Row	Total Number of Tiles
1	1
2	4
3	9
4	?
5	?
6	?
7	?

ON YOUR OWN

1. The first four triangular numbers are shown below. Copy and complete the table. How can you describe the pattern? Write a rule for the pattern.

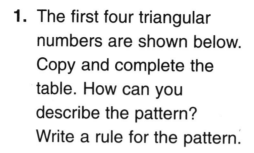

Design Number	Total Number of Dots
1	1
2	3
3	6
4	10
5	?
6	?
7	?
8	?
9	?

2. *My Journal:* Was this pattern difficult for you to find? Explain your thinking.

Practise Your Skills

1. Copy and complete the T-table.

2. How much money would be earned in 10 hours? in 15 hours?

Number of Hours	Money Earned
1	$ 7.00
2	$ 14.00
3	$ 21.00
4	?
5	?

Write the next three numbers in each pattern.

3. 5, 9, 13, 17, …

4. 96, 84, 72, 60, …

Graphing Patterns

▶ Describe the patterns you see in each table.
How many **triangles** are needed for Design Number 8?
How many **parallelograms** are needed for Design Number 8?
Copy and complete each table to help you find out.

Design Number	Number of Triangles
1	4
2	8
3	12
4	?
5	?
6	?
7	?
8	?

Design Number	Number of Parallelograms
1	2
2	6
3	12
4	?
5	?
6	?
7	?
8	?

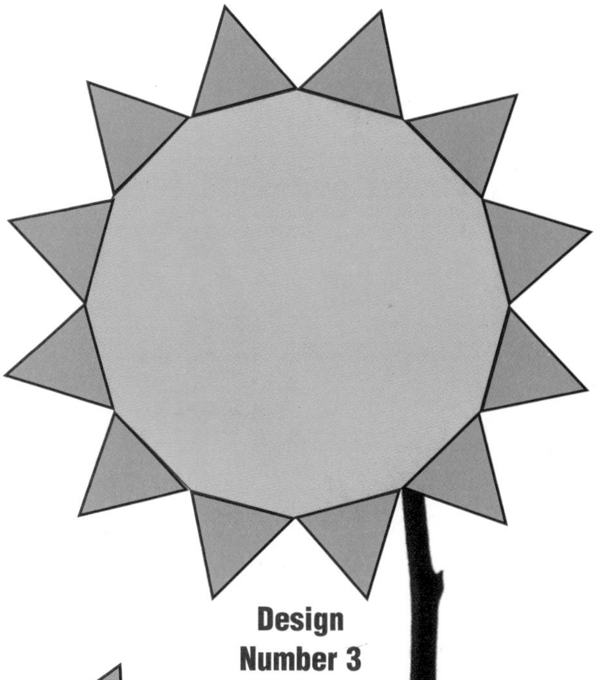

Design Number 3

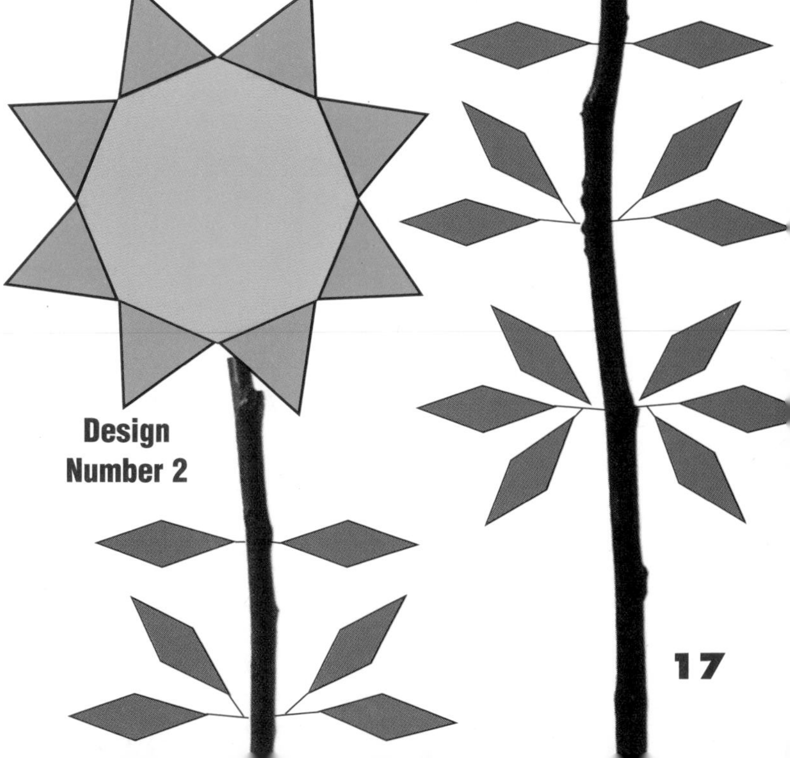

Design Number 2

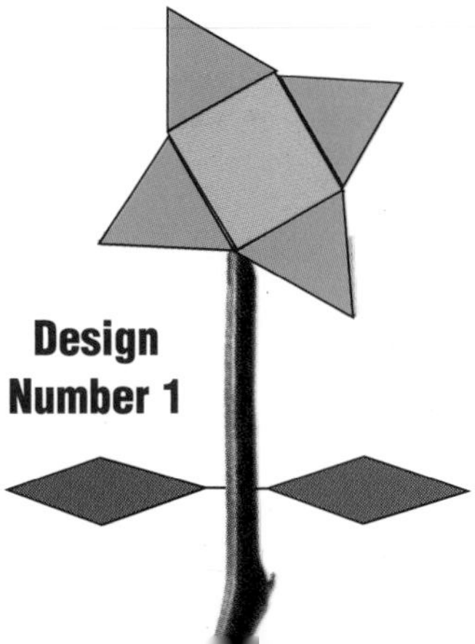

Design Number 1

How do you plot points?

1 You can write or think about a T-table using **ordered pairs**.

Quantity 1	Quantity 2		
1	2	→	(1, 2)
2	3	→	(2, 3)
3	4	→	(3, 4)
4	5	→	(4, 5)
5	6	→	(5, 6)
6	7	→	(6, 7)

These are ordered pairs.

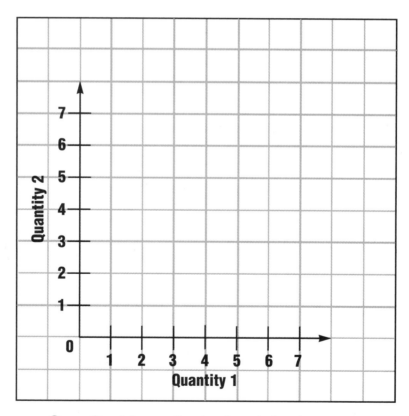

Quantity 1 is on the horizontal axis.
Quantity 2 is on the vertical axis.

2 You can plot ordered pairs on a grid.

Start at 0.

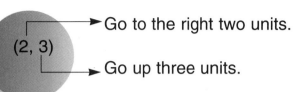

(2, 3) → Go to the right two units.

→ Go up three units.

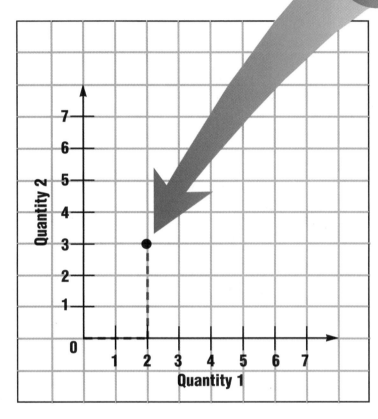

Quantity 2

Quantity 1

3 Look at the pattern formed when you plot the rest of the points.

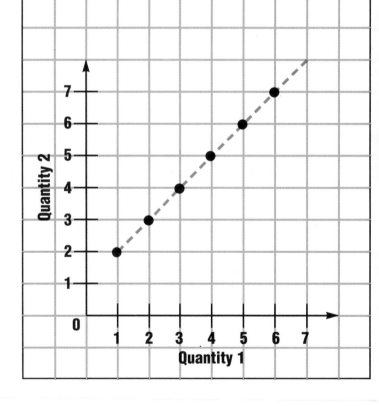

Quantity 2

Quantity 1

It's easy. Just follow the steps!

ON YOUR OWN

1. Look at this pattern. Copy and complete the T-table. Then use grid paper to graph the data.

   Suppose you used 10 hexagons. How many triangles would you need?

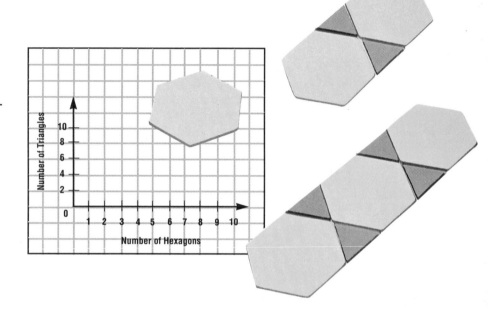

Number of Hexagons	Number of Triangles
1	0
2	2
3	4
4	?
5	?
6	?

2. *My Journal:* What have you learned about coordinate graphing?

Practise Your Skills

	Quantity 1	Quantity 2
1. Graph the data in this T-table.	1	3
	2	6
2. When Quantity 1 is 12, what is Quantity 2?	3	9
	4	?
	5	?
	6	?

Using Data to Predict

▶ About how long do you think it would take the students in the picture to pass the hand squeeze?

ON YOUR OWN

1. Copy and complete the table below. Use grid paper. Draw a line graph for these data. Use the graph to predict the time for 25, 30, and 35 hand squeezes.

Number of squeezes	5	10	15	20	25	30	35
Time needed to make squeezes (in seconds)	4	8	12	16	?	?	?

2. What do you think would happen in the hand-squeezing experiment if you waited a week and tried it again? What would happen if you did it with your eyes closed? Try it. Was your prediction true?

3. *My Journal:* When are line graphs helpful? Explain.

Practíse Your Skills

1. Copy and complete the table for this pattern. Extend the table for five more columns.

Perimeter (units)	4	8	12	16	?	?
Area (square units)	1	4	9	?	?	?

Recognizing Rules for Number Pairs

▶ What is the Input/Output rule for each Number Cruncher machine?

Use the rules to make up five more Input/Output number pairs for each machine.

Crunchers can also "crunch" polygons. How is each Cruncher "crunching" the input polygons?

1.

2.

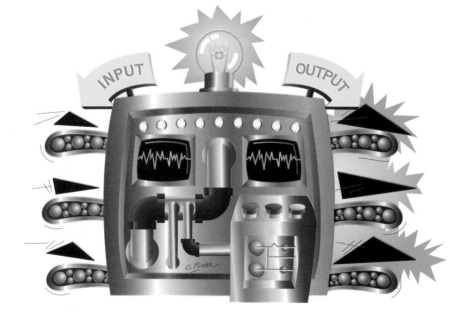

Rule:
Multiply the first number by 2.
Add the second number.

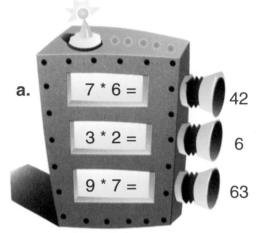

3. What rule is used?

2 * 1 =		5
3 * 4 =		10
0 * 2 =		2

a.

7 * 6 =		42
3 * 2 =		6
9 * 7 =		63

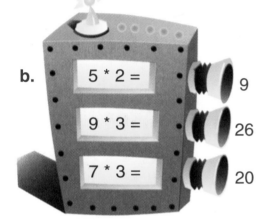

b.

5 * 2 =		9
9 * 3 =		26
7 * 3 =		20

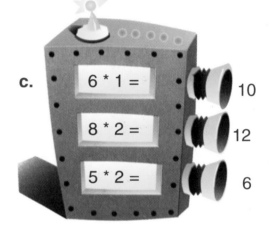

c.

6 * 1 =		10
8 * 2 =		12
5 * 2 =		6

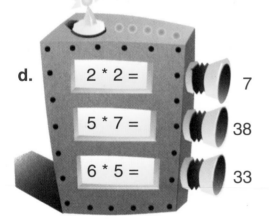

d.

2 * 2 =		7
5 * 7 =		38
6 * 5 =		33

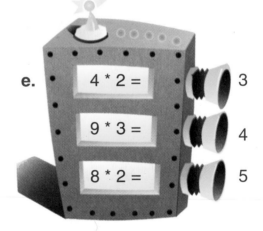

e.

4 * 2 =		3
9 * 3 =		4
8 * 2 =		5

4. Make up your own rule. Write several examples using your rule. See if someone else can find your rule.

5. *My Journal:* What have you learned about inputs, patterns, and outputs?

Going Around in
CIRCLES, SQUARES,
and TRIANGLES

Have you ever wondered what number patterns people think are interesting, and why? Interest in mathematical patterns is not restricted to any one culture. People from Africa, China, Japan, the Middle East, Tibet, and elsewhere have experimented with number patterns. Some number patterns even take on geometric shapes.

Tibetan Number Square

Lo-Shu

Chinese Number Square

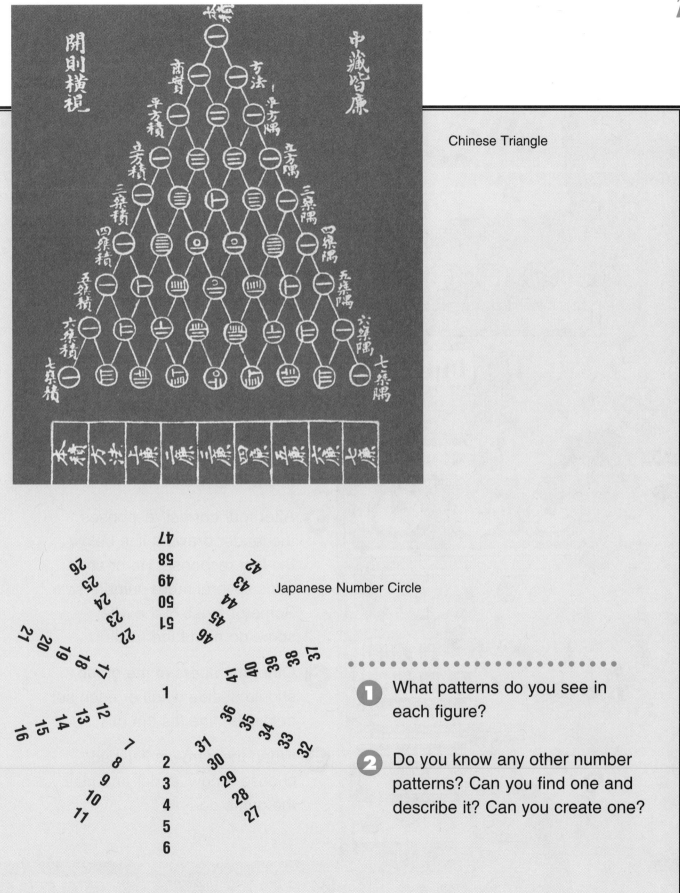

Chinese Triangle

Japanese Number Circle

· ·

1 What patterns do you see in each figure?

2 Do you know any other number patterns? Can you find one and describe it? Can you create one?

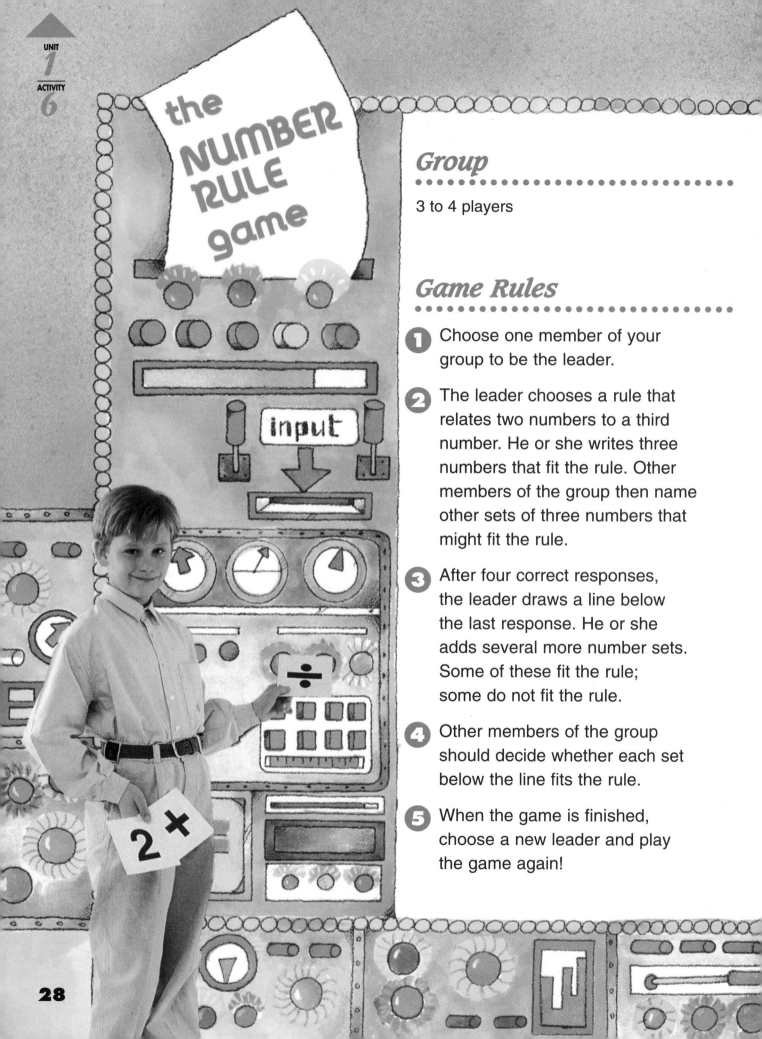

the NUMBER RULE game

Group

3 to 4 players

Game Rules

1 Choose one member of your group to be the leader.

2 The leader chooses a rule that relates two numbers to a third number. He or she writes three numbers that fit the rule. Other members of the group then name other sets of three numbers that might fit the rule.

3 After four correct responses, the leader draws a line below the last response. He or she adds several more number sets. Some of these fit the rule; some do not fit the rule.

4 Other members of the group should decide whether each set below the line fits the rule.

5 When the game is finished, choose a new leader and play the game again!

1. What is the rule that relates the first two numbers to the third number for each set of data?

A

2	2	5
3	2	7
4	2	9
8	2	17
10	4	41

B

4	2	1
9	5	2
7	1	3
12	4	4
15	3	6

2. Which of these sets fit the rule for A?

3	5	9
6	2	12
1	0	1

3. Which of these sets fit the rule for B?

4	0	2
8	3	3
16	4	6

Patterns and T-Tables

▶ Which would you rather be paid?
- one million dollars, or
- one cent the first day, two cents the second day, four cents the third day, and so on, doubling the number of cents each day for one month

GET RICH QUICK!

$ $ $ $ $ $ $ $ $ $ $ $ $

Double Your Money Daily!

$ $ $ $ $ $ $ $ $ $ $ $ $

Start with only

1¢

September

1   2   4

7   8   9   10   11

Plant Tree!

14   15   16   17   18

21   22   23   24   2

28   29   30

WIN A MILLION DOLLARS IN ONE MONTH!

BIG BUCKS DOLLAR DRIVE   123
PAY TO THE
ORDER OF   Your Name Here! $1000 000
One Million Dollars   00
                                      100

MAIL
¢

To Resident
1212 National Lane
Anytown, Canada

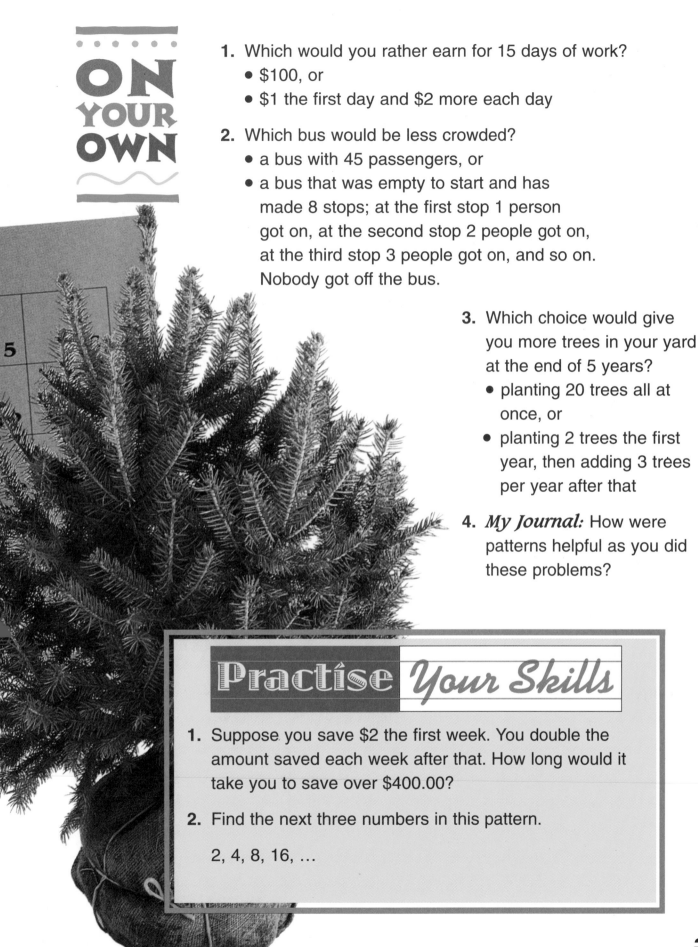

1. Which would you rather earn for 15 days of work?
   - $100, or
   - $1 the first day and $2 more each day

2. Which bus would be less crowded?
   - a bus with 45 passengers, or
   - a bus that was empty to start and has made 8 stops; at the first stop 1 person got on, at the second stop 2 people got on, at the third stop 3 people got on, and so on. Nobody got off the bus.

3. Which choice would give you more trees in your yard at the end of 5 years?
   - planting 20 trees all at once, or
   - planting 2 trees the first year, then adding 3 trees per year after that

4. *My Journal:* How were patterns helpful as you did these problems?

Practise Your Skills

1. Suppose you save $2 the first week. You double the amount saved each week after that. How long would it take you to save over $400.00?

2. Find the next three numbers in this pattern.

   2, 4, 8, 16, …

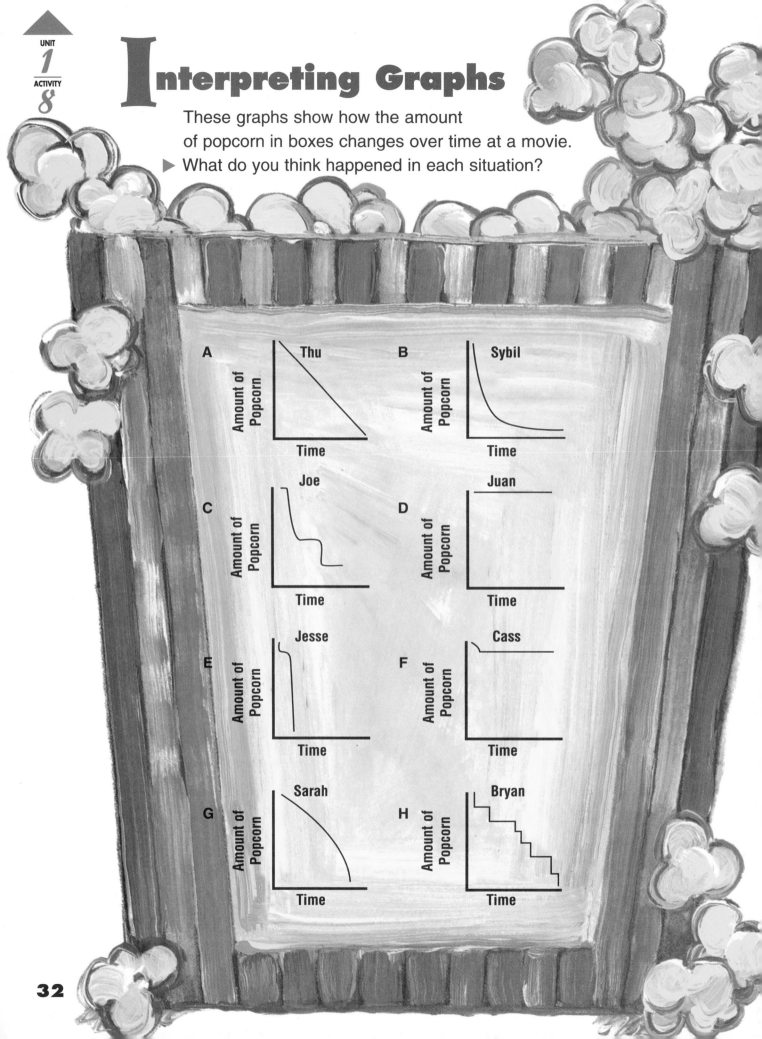

Interpreting Graphs

These graphs show how the amount
of popcorn in boxes changes over time at a movie.

▶ What do you think happened in each situation?

A — Thu

B — Sybil

C — Joe

D — Juan

E — Jesse

F — Cass

G — Sarah

H — Bryan

UNIT 1
ACTIVITY 8

Which activity do you think describes which graph?
Explain your reasoning.

1. Number of people watching television at a given time

2. Number of students doing homework at a given time

3. Number of people at a shopping mall at a given time

4. Number of people eating a meal at a given time

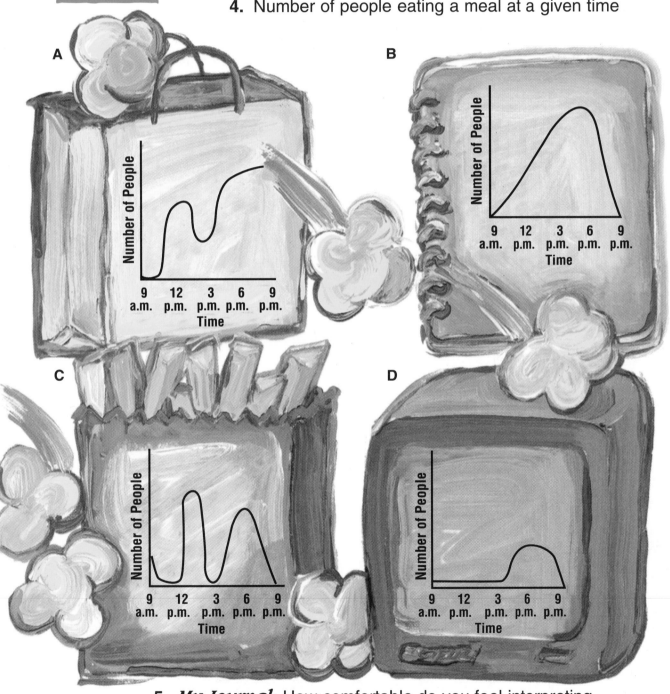

5. *My Journal:* How comfortable do you feel interpreting
graphs that show relationships? Explain.

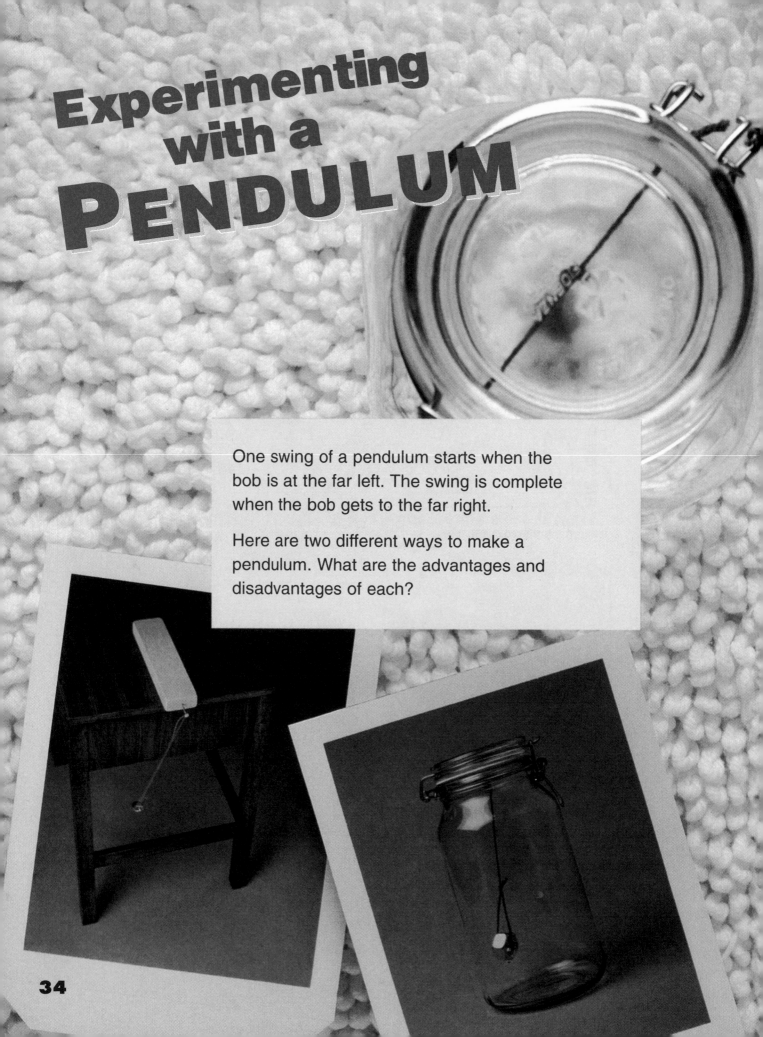

Experimenting with a PENDULUM

One swing of a pendulum starts when the bob is at the far left. The swing is complete when the bob gets to the far right.

Here are two different ways to make a pendulum. What are the advantages and disadvantages of each?

Make a pendulum of your own.
Use it to do some experiments. For each
experiment, create a data table and
record your results in a graph.

- How many times does the pendulum
  swing in 15 seconds?

- How long does it take for one swing?

- Is the time the same if you change:
  the weight of the bob?
  the length of the string?
  the width of the swing?

- Create an experiment of your own.
  Decide what you are testing. Predict
  what will happen. Then experiment to
  see if your prediction was correct!

CheckYOURSELF

Great job! You made a pendulum and used it for
some experiments. Your plans, data, and results were
clearly written for each experiment. You used data
tables and graphs to show your results. You wrote
to explain how data tables and graphs were used in your
experiments.

PROBLEM BANK

1. Calendars have interesting number properties.

   a. Add all seven numbers in any row. Divide the sum by 7. Look for your answer among the numbers in that row. Repeat this procedure for another row. Describe any pattern you find.

   b. Choose four numbers on your calendar that form a square. Multiply the numbers at diagonally opposite corners. Subtract the smaller product from the larger. What do you discover?

JULY						
	1	2	3	4	5	6
7	8	9	10	11	12	13
14	15	16	17	18	19	20
21	22	23	24	25	26	27

   c. Find and describe other interesting number patterns on a calendar.

2. For baby-sitting, Andrea charges $3.00 for every hour before midnight. She charges a higher rate for every hour after midnight. The table shows the times she began and finished on two occasions and the amount she charged each time.

Began at	Finished at	Charged
7:00 p.m.	1:00 a.m.	$19.00
8:00 p.m.	2:00 a.m.	$20.00

Suppose Andrea began at 9:00 p.m. and finished at 2:00 a.m. How much would she charge? Show how you arrived at your answer.

3. Naveen is entering a Terry Fox walkathon to raise money for cancer research. His sponsor can contribute $20 for his walk or $5 plus $2 for every kilometre that he walks. How far must Naveen walk to receive a contribution greater than $20?

4. Janet folded a large piece of tissue paper in half. The fold divided the paper into halves. She folded it in half again. When she unfolded it, the folds divided the paper into quarters. She continued to fold and unfold the paper until the folds divided it into 128 equal parts. How many times did Janet fold the paper? Use a T-table.

SKILL BANK FROM THIS UNIT

1. Write the next three numbers in each pattern.

a. 1, 3, 5, 7, ■, ■, ■

b. 6, 13, 20, 27, ■, ■, ■

c. 33, 30, 27, 24, ■, ■, ■

d. 3, 9, 27, 81, ■, ■, ■

2. Examine the input and output numbers in each T-table. Find the rule for each. Copy and complete each table. Graph the ordered pairs.

a.

Input	Output
2	6
3	9
4	12
5	15
6	18
7	?
8	?
9	?

b.

Input	Output
2	9
4	11
6	13
8	15
10	17
12	?
14	?
16	?

c.

Input	Output
2	2
3	4
4	6
5	8
6	10
7	?
8	?
9	?

d.

Input	Output
2	4
3	9
4	14
5	19
6	24
7	?
8	?
9	?

3. **a.** Make a T-table for this pattern.

   b. How many squares would there be in the 10th design?

| 2 | 6 | 12 | 20 |

4. Write the next three numbers in each pattern.

   a. 5, 6, 8, 11, 15, 20, ■, ■, ■

   b. 100, 98, 94, 88, 80, 70, ■, ■, ■

   c. 2, 4, 8, 14, 22, 32, ■, ■, ■

   d. 50, 49, 47, 44, 40, 35, ■, ■, ■

5. **a.** Copy and complete the T-table.

   b. Graph the ordered pairs.

   c. How many diagonals does a decagon have?

Number of Sides	Number of Diagonals
3	0
4	?
5	?
6	?

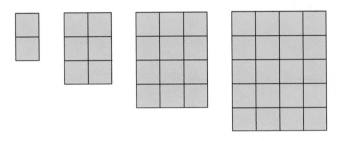

1151 race to fill 500 starting positions

Young Girl Dashes 1000 Metres in Record Time

105 300 Line Marathon Route

CROSS COUNTRY RACE DRAWS CROWD OF 13 500

17 500 Runners Raise $600 000 for Charity

How can we describe numbers?

REPRESENTING NUMBERS

STARTING OUT

1
- Which vehicle is the most expensive?
- Which vehicle is the least expensive?
- Which vehicles are priced between $5000 and $10 000?
- Which vehicles have prices that differ by $500 or less?
- Which vehicles are priced at over $10 000?

My Journal: What do you know about reading and writing numbers greater than 999?

REPRESENTING NUMBERS

S·T·A·R·T·I·N·G OUT

TEN THOUSANDS	THOUSANDS	HUNDREDS	TENS	ONES
9	0	8	2	6

2 ● What number does each picture show?
 ● What is the greatest number on these pages?
 ● What is the least number on these pages?
 ● Why is it important to know how to read numbers?

My Journal: What do you know about comparing numbers greater than 999?

Visualizing Numbers

► Estimate the number shown by each group of blocks. Then find the number. Record it in numerals and in words.

1.

2.

3.

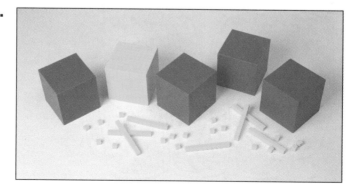

ON YOUR OWN

1. Write five numbers between 3225 and 6085.
   Draw base ten blocks to show each number.
   Record each number in words.

2. What is the least number of base ten blocks you could
   use to represent 5840? What is the greatest number
   of blocks you could use? Explain your thinking.

3. What number do these blocks represent?

   a. Write a number that is 3000 less.
   b. Write a number that is 700 greater.
   c. Write a number that is 40 less.
   d. Write a number that is 8 greater.

4. *My Journal:* What do you know about the
   relationships among base ten blocks?

Practise *Your Skills*

Write each numeral in words.
   1. 5197   **2.** 8306   **3.** 3027   **4.** 7080

Write the numeral for each.
   5. nine thousand eight hundred six
   6. seven hundred eighty-nine
   7. seven thousand fifty-eight
   8. 5000 + 700 + 90 + 2
   9. 8000 + 10 + 8
   10. 2000 + 800 + 60

Visualizing Hundred Thousands

Here are the populations of eight cities.

Wide River	16 208
Whoville	198 417
Hickory Hollow	2 147
Hilltop	433 212
Peterpatch	25 380
Lakeside City	476 352
Grassburg	215 149
Pine Valley	6 380

1. Make a place value chart. Write each population on the chart.

2. Write each population in words.

3. List the cities in order from least to greatest population.

4. Beantown has a population of 321 040. Where would it fit in your list?

5. Round each population
   • to the nearest thousand,
   • to the nearest ten thousand, and
   • to the nearest hundred thousand (where possible).

ON YOUR OWN

Write one number for each problem. Use base ten blocks or a place value chart to help you.

1. What number could it be?
   - It is between 12 000 and 13 000.
   - Its hundreds, tens, and ones digits are all odd.
   - The sum of all its digits is 12.

2. What number could it be?
   - It is greater than 900 000 and less than 999 999.
   - The sum of all its digits is 35.
   - Its thousands digit and its ones digit are the same.
   - Its tens digit is odd.

3. What number could it be?
   - It is between 125 000 and 130 000.
   - It contains all the numbers from 0 to 5.
   - Its thousands digit is two more than its tens digit.
   - Its hundreds digit is even.

4. *My Journal:* How do you compare numbers?

Practise Your Skills

Write each numeral in words.
1. 20 682   2. 433 000   3. 169 080   4. 207 350

Write each number in exercises 5 and 6 as a numeral.
5. twenty-six thousand one hundred nine

6. six hundred seventeen thousand three hundred fifty-six

7. Count by hundreds from 27 600 to 28 000.

8. Count by tens from 399 970 to 400 020.

The CALCULATOR Place Value Game

Group

3 to 4 players

Materials

• calculators

Game Rules

1 Players sit in a circle. Players name themselves A, B, C, D around the circle.

2 Each player keys in a five-digit numeral on the calculator without letting the other players see it.

3 Player A asks Player B for any digit from 1 to 9. If Player B has that digit in her or his calculator display:
  • Player B says the number that digit represents;
  • Player B subtracts that number from her or his total;
  • Player A adds that number to his or her total; and
  • Player A takes another turn with Player C.

If Player B does not have that digit, then Player B asks Player C for any digit from 1 to 9.

4 Play continues around the circle as described in 3.

5 When a player reaches 0 on the calculator display, that player is out of the game, and the remaining players keep playing.

6 Play continues until one player is left in the game or until a predetermined time limit has been reached.

Roman Numerals

Have you ever seen numbers written in a way that is different from the way you write them?

In ancient Egypt, ∩ meant 10. \ meant 1. In Babylonia, < meant 10 and V meant 1. You might have seen these markings to represent 22:

\\ ∩∩   or   << VV

Roman numerals are another way to show numbers. They are still used today. You might see them on buildings, on clocks, and in books. Here are some of the symbols that make up the Roman numeral system:

I = 1   V = 5   X = 10
L = 50   C = 100   D = 500
M = 1000

A bar on top of a Roman numeral shows thousands, so V with a bar on top is 5000 and X with a bar on top is 10 000.

The Roman system uses subtraction to represent numbers. The number 4 is written as IV — one less than 5. The system also uses a shortcut — you never use more than three of the same symbol in a row. Here are the numbers 1 to 20, in order:

I,   II,   III,   IV,   V,
VI,   VII,   VIII,   IX,   X,
XI,   XII,   XIII,   XIV,   XV,
XVI, XVII, XVIII, XIX,   XX.

- -

1 Explain something you find interesting about the Roman numeral system.

2 Choose three numbers greater than 100. Write them in Roman numerals. Ask a friend to figure out what the numbers are.

3 How is the Roman system like the system you use? How is it different? Explain which one you think is better, and why.

Developing Number Sense

▶ Suppose you started reading novels when you were ten years old. You read one thousand pages a month. About how old would you be when you finished reading one million pages?

BUILDING A MODEL FOR 1 000 000

What to do:

- Think about the cube-rod-flat pattern used in base ten blocks.

- You don't have 1 million cubes. So, what can you do to represent 1 million cubes?

- Work with the members of your group. Decide on the shape and dimensions for your model of 1 000 000. Write to explain how you decided on the shape of your model and how you know it shows 1 000 000.

Materials
you might use:

- metre sticks

- base ten blocks

- centimetre grid paper

- scissors and masking tape

- big pieces of cardboard,
  tagboard, cardboard tubes,
  or dowels made from newspaper

Discuss these questions in your group.

1. Imagine you build a box that can hold one million
   centimetre cubes. About how many people
   your size could fit inside the box?

2. Would one million pairs of roller blades fit inside your
   classroom? would one million bicycles?

3. About how many marbles would fit inside a compact car?

*C*heck**Y**OURSELF

Great job! Your one million model shows a clear
understanding of place value. You communicated
your ideas well and showed clear thinking.

PROBLEM BANK

1. The Martindales removed the house number from their front door so that they could paint the door. What could the house number be? List all the possibilities.

2. Arrange each set of digits below to make
   - the least possible number
   - the greatest possible number
   - a number that falls between the least and greatest.

   a. 2 9 3 8 6 5   **b.** 4 5 9 4 0
   c. 6 2 7 3 0 4   **d.** 7 8 6 1 5

3. Round each number to the nearest 10 000. Explain how you rounded.
   a. 86 342   **b.** 197 408   **c.** 620 513

4. **a.** Which class collected the most bread tags?
   b. Which classes collected between 5000 and 10 000 bread tags?
   c. Which two classes combined collected about as many tags as the class that collected the most?
   d. About how many bread tags were collected in all?

Bread Tags Collected This Year	
Room 1	2 685
Room 2	10 362
Room 3	4 907
Room 4	8 647
Room 5	3 518
Room 6	12 485
Room 7	7 345

5. Record the next three numbers in each pattern.

   a. 8000, 16 000, 24 000, 32 000, ■, ■, ■

   b. 19 032, 21 032, 23 032, 25 032, ■, ■, ■

   c. 24 100, 24 150, 24 200, 24 250, ■, ■, ■

6. Order these video game scores from least to greatest.
Explain how you decided on the order.

   26 945   85 327   38 042   90 000   14 131

7. Suppose you won $1 000 000. How many bills would you
get if you were paid in:

   a. $1000 bills   **b.** $100 bills   **c.** $10 bills

8. How many boxes of staples would you need to buy
to get each number?

   a. 10 000

   b. 100 000

   c. 12 500

   d. 1 000 000

9. Ask a classmate to count the number of times you blink in
one minute. Use this number to estimate the number of
times you blink in:

   a. one hour   **b.** one day   **c.** one week

10. Choose a book. Estimate the number of words in it.
Count the words on one page and use this number
to make a second estimate.

SKILL BANK
FROM THIS UNIT

1. Write the numeral for each.
   a. ninety thousand five hundred sixty
   b. one thousand four hundred nine
   c. three hundred thousand
   d. ten thousand one hundred
   e. 3000 + 600 + 7
   f. 7000 + 20 + 2
   g. 10 000 + 500
   h. 80 000 + 3000 + 100

2. Write each numeral in words.
   a. 7490
   b. 10 456
   c. 87 600
   d. 101 670

3. Count by ones from 38 695 to 38 705.

4. Count by thousands from 17 600 to 21 600.

5. State the value of each underlined digit.
   a. 74<u>9</u>0
   b. <u>10</u> 456
   c. 87 <u>6</u>00
   d. 10<u>1</u> 670

6. Record the greater number in each pair.
   a. 65 600 or 66 500
   b. 709 578 or 709 758
   c. 129 734 or 219 743

7. Order each set of numbers from least to greatest.
   a. 61 208, 60 802, 61 200
   b. 231 822, 213 839, 231 834

8. a. Use the digits 8, 4, 0, 5, 2 to make the least number possible.
   b. Use the same digits to make the greatest number possible.

9. a. Which number is closest to 497 800?
   b. Which number is 500 less than 497 800?
   c. Which number is 1 more than 828 499?
   d. Which number is 8000 more than 111 000?

   497 300   828 500
   119 000   492 800
   119 800   829 500

1. Find the rule for each T-table. Copy and complete the table. Graph the ordered pairs.

Input	Output
17	8
16	7
15	6
14	5
13	?
12	?
11	?

Input	Output
2	8
3	11
4	14
5	17
13	?
12	?
11	?

2. Write the next three numbers in the pattern.
   a. 10, 11, 13, 16, 20, ■, ■, ■
   b. 2, 5, 3, 6, 4, 7, 5, ■, ■, ■
   c. 3, 6, 12, 24, 48, ■, ■, ■

3. Write the numeral for each.
   a. one hundred ten thousand one hundred
   b. sixty thousand sixteen
   c. eight thousand two
   d. 10 000 + 400 + 8
   e. 70 000 + 5000 + 20

4. **a.** What number is 1 more than 16 999?
   b. What number is 1000 more than 239 847?
   c. What number is 1 less than 213 000?
   d. What number is 100 less than 68 724?
   e. Which is closer to 65 000: 67 200 or 63 200?

UNIT

3

**Reasoning
with
Operations**

*H*ow can we use operations?

61

REASONING WITH OPERATIONS

S·T·A·R·T·I·N·G

S **OUT**

1 • Describe how addition, subtraction, multiplication, or division are used in these pictures.

• What other photograph could be added to this page? Explain how operations would be used in the scene you add.

• Write some problems based on the information you see here. Make sure that operations could be used to solve them.

5¢ a day
for
overdue books

Tuesday
June
7

My Journal: Which operations were easy
to use? Why do you think that?

2 • Estimate how much it will cost this family to see the movie. About how much change will they have from two $20 bills?

• What snacks can this family buy with the money they have left over?

• Which of the combination deals do you think is best? Explain your thinking.

• Suppose you were to go to a movie with your family. How much would it cost based on the price list you see here? Would that be more or less than for the family here? Why do you think that?

• Suppose renting a video costs $4.00. Popcorn for your family costs $2.00. Drinks are $1.00 each. Would it be cheaper for your family to go out to a movie or to stay in and rent a video? Explain your thinking. Why might you choose one over the other, no matter what it cost?

• Write some problems using any of the information you see here. Use at least two operations in each problem. Challenge a friend to solve the problems.

My Journal: Which operation do you use most often? Why do you think that is?

COMING ATTRACTIONS

Large	Regular	Small
3.75	3.25	2.50
2.75	2.50	2.00
3.00	2.00	1.50

COMBO DEALS

Large Popcorn & Large Drink $6.25

Large Popcorn & 2 Small Drinks $7.00

Regular Popcorn & 2 Regular Drinks $7.25

BOX OFFICE

Ticket Prices

$ 8.00 Adults
$ 6.50 Youths
$ 4.25 Children

Exploring Factors and Multiples

▶ How many tiles were used to build this rectangle?

3 x 4 = 12
↓   ↓
factor factor

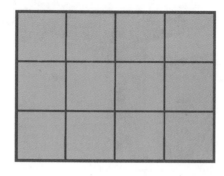

- What other rectangles can be built with 12 tiles?
- What are the factors of 12?

▶ How many tiles were used to build this rectangle?

- What are the factors of 11?

Words to Know

Factors:	the numbers multiplied in a multiplication expression
Multiple:	a number that is the product of a given whole number and another whole number
Prime Number:	any whole number greater than 1 that has only two factors (1 and itself)
Composite Number:	any whole number greater than 1 that has more than two factors

ON YOUR OWN

Use any methods to solve these problems.

1. There are 36 students in the Art Club. They need to work in equal-sized groups on a project. What groupings are possible?

2. Suppose 6 more students join the Art Club. What equal groupings are possible now?

3. The number of students in the Camera Club has 2, 4, 6, and 8 as some of its factors. How many students might there be in the Camera Club?

4. *My Journal:* When might you use what you know about factors in real situations?

Practise Your Skills

1. List all the factors of each number below.

2. Which of the numbers below are prime numbers?

3. Which of the numbers are multiples of 7?

70   48

96   55   28   100

67   76   35

Using Operations

▶ Use this menu. Decide how many pizzas and soft drinks to order for a class party.

~PIZZAS~

Large	(8 slices)	$12.95
Small	(4 slices)	$9.75
Each Topping		$0.25

Toppings

Sausages, Pepperoni, Mushroom, Onions, Olives, Green Pepper

~Soft Drinks~

| 6 Packs | $2.99 |
| Case (24 cans) | $7.50 |

Sorry, no single cans or slices

1. For each expression, write a story problem that might be solved by doing that calculation. Then solve the problem. Show all your work.

   a. 3×28

   b. $18 + 28 + 16$

   c. $85 - 13$

   d. $16 \div 4$

2. *My Journal:* What have you learned about choosing operations to solve a problem?

Practise Your Skills

1. 85×6	**2.** 3×58	**3.** 68×10	**4.** 400×7
5. $52 \div 7$	**6.** $34 \div 5$	**7.** $84 \div 3$	**8.** $51 \div 4$
9. $98 + 69$	**10.** $168 + 21$	**11.** $522 + 698$	**12.** $436 + 3581$
13. $69 - 47$	**14.** $743 - 580$	**15.** $238 - 59$	**16.** $1413 - 297$

Equal Shares

I eat my peas with honey.
I've done it all my life.
It makes the peas taste funny.
But it keeps them on the knife.

▶ How can 7 people share 24 peas?

Modelling Multiplication

Here are two ways to show the product of 13 by 15.

▶ What is the total number of squares?

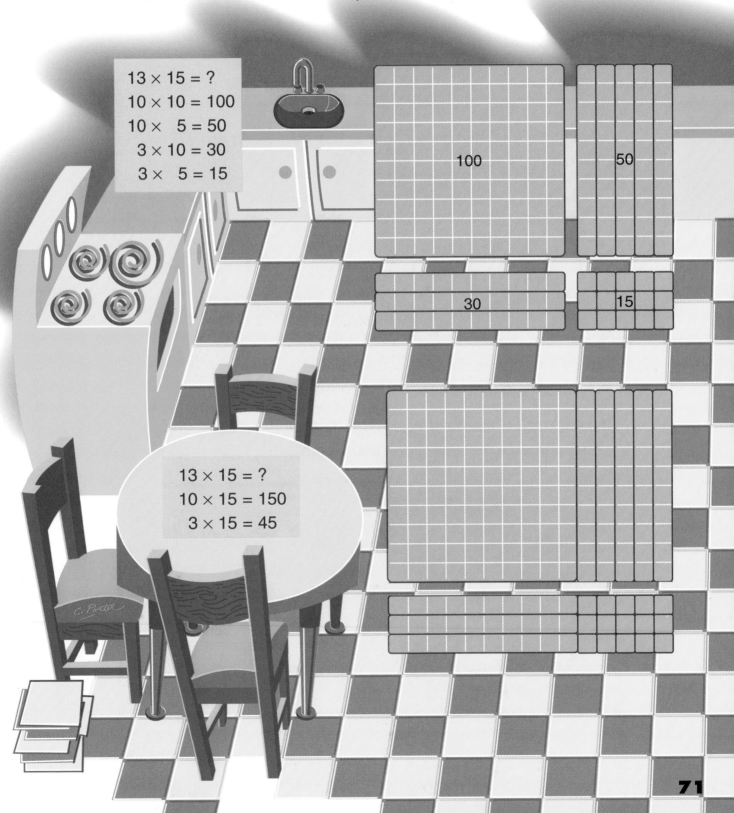

$13 \times 15 = ?$
$10 \times 10 = 100$
$10 \times 5 = 50$
$3 \times 10 = 30$
$3 \times 5 = 15$

$13 \times 15 = ?$
$10 \times 15 = 150$
$3 \times 15 = 45$

ON YOUR OWN

1. Write four multiplication expressions for these arrays. Show that they have the same total as 14×23.

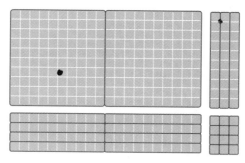

2. What is the total number of small squares in each array? How did you find it?

a. 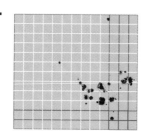   b.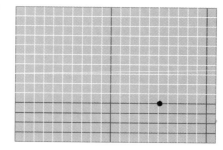

3. Sketch an array to show 13×22. Write multiplication expressions to explain the array.

4. *My Journal:* What have you learned about multiplying and partial products that you didn't know before?

Practise Your Skills

Multiply.

1. 3×6	**2.** 4×5	**3.** 5×300	**4.** 20×20
3×70	4×30	5×30	20×5
3×76	4×200	5×3	8×5
	4×235	5×333	8×20
			28×25

THE TARGET GAME

Group

2 players

Materials

- recording sheets
- calculator

Liam			Margot		
Target	Multiplication	Difference Score	Target	Multiplication	Difference Score
400	35 x 12 = 420	20	400	15 x 29 = 435	35
1200			1200		

Game Rules

1 Each pair chooses a game board.

2 Each player chooses a number from each column on the game board and records them as factors in a multiplication expression. Players try to choose numbers whose product will be as close to the target number on that game board as possible. Once a player records the two numbers, they cannot be changed.

3 Each player multiplies her or his two numbers to find the product.

4 Players compare their products and estimate which is closer to the target number on the game board.

5 Each player finds the difference between her or his product and the target number, and records this as her or his score.

6 Players use calculators to settle any disagreements.

7 Players choose another game board and continue play. The player with the lower total score after five rounds is the winner.

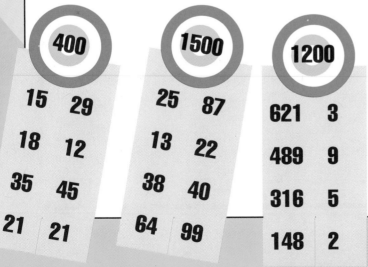

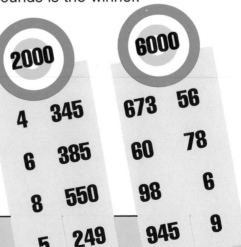

400	1500	1200	2000	6000
15 29	25 87	621 3	4 345	673 56
18 12	13 22	489 9	6 385	60 78
35 45	38 40	316 5	8 550	98 6
21 21	64 99	148 2	5 249	945 9

1. Write multiplication statements for parts of each array. How can you find the total for each array? What is each total?

a.

b.

2. Write a multiplication expression for each situation. Find the product.

a. the number of hours you are at school in one month

b. the number of times you brush your teeth in one year

c. the number of trips you make between school and home in one year

d. the number of minutes you spend at recess in one month

e. the number of minutes you spend learning math in one week

3. Find each product in two ways. Show all your work.

a. 36×58 **b.** 452×26

4. *My Journal:* What questions do you have about multiplying?

Practise Your Skills

1. Multiply.

a.	**b.**	**c.**	**d.**
3×4	2×8	80×40	30×80
10×4	30×8	80×3	30×5
13×4	32×8	2×40	7×80
		2×3	7×5
		82×43	37×85

2. Estimate. Then find each product.

a. 34×26 **b.** 98×33 **c.** 212×45 **d.** 76×327

UNIT
3
ACTIVITY
5

odelling Division

Here are four arrays. Part of each array is missing.
Find how many cubes there should be in each
column or row.

▶ Use base ten blocks to model the complete array for
each number. Sketch the array.

▶ Write a division expression that describes the array.
Include remainders if there are cubes left over.

1. 162 cubes
9 columns

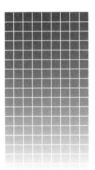

2. 230 cubes
7 rows

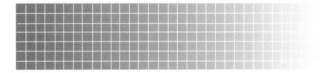

3. 243 cubes
9 columns

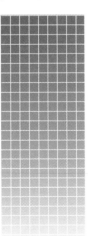

4. 192 cubes
8 rows

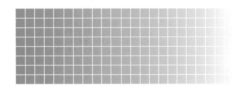

1. Start with 75 cubes. How many are in each row if there are 5 rows? 12 rows? 25 rows?

2. Suppose you want to build a rectangle with 12 rows and have a remainder of 5. How many cubes must you start with? Find at least two ways to solve the problem. Record each solution.

3. Write a division expression for each situation. Then find the number.
   a. the number of Mondays in one year
   b. the number of weeks in 185 days
   c. the number of nickels in $8
   d. the number of years in 60 months
   e. the number of $2 coins in a $50 roll

4. *My Journal:* What have you learned about finding the number of cubes in the rows and columns of an array?

Practise Your Skills

1. Use division to determine whether each statement is true.
   a. $238 \times 4 = 952$ b. $56 \times 9 = 504$ c. $7 \times 133 = 931$

2. Use multiplication to determine whether each statement is true.
   a. $875 \div 5 = 175$ b. $588 \div 6 = 98$ c. $7 \overline{)476}$ with 68 above

Explaining Multiplication and Division

▶ Find each product or quotient. Record all your work so you can explain to others how you multiply and divide.

36×12 $75 \div 8$

157×40 $45 \div 4$

124×5 $355 \div 6$

▶ Think about how these students multiply and divide.
What questions do you have?

Chalkboard Talk
36×12

36 × 10 = 360
36 × 2 = 72
360 + 72 = 432
36 × 12 = 432

45 ÷ 4

4 × 11 = 44 (4 groups of 11)
45 − 44 = 1 (1 left over)
45 ÷ 4 = 11 R1

▶ For each expression, write a story problem that might be solved by doing that calculation. Then solve each problem. Show all your work.

1. 7×38
2. 25×25
3. $365 \div 5$
4. 567×4
5. $67 \div 9$

ON YOUR OWN

1. Write a note or draw a picture to explain to someone that $34 \times 56 = 1904$.

2. Write a note to someone explaining how you can use multiplication to prove that $320 \div 8 = 40$.

3. Sketch an array to explain the product of 24×38.

4. Find a missing number that results in a product in the range shown.

a.

$40 \times$ ___ Range:

b.

$455 \times$ ___ Range:

c.

$78 \times$ ___ Range:
650
750

d.

$15 \times$ ___ Range:
950
1000

5. Arrange the digits 2, 3, 4, and 5 to make the greatest product possible.

___ ___ × ___ ___   or   ___ ___ ___ × ___

6. Arrange the digits 2, 4, 6, and 8 to make the least product possible.

___ ___ × ___ ___   or   ___ ___ ___ × ___

7. *My Journal:* How are strategies for multiplication and division related?

Estimate, then calculate.

1. 901×30 **2.** 436×5 **3.** 982×3

4. 92×63 **5.** 81×95 **6.** 774×48

7. $46 \div 4$ **8.** $77 \div 3$ **9.** $921 \div 8$

10. $7\overline{)918}$ **11.** $2\overline{)708}$ **12.** $7\overline{)570}$

Solving Problems

▶ Yodos, Modos, and Hodos are teams in Boboball. This is a version of soccer known only to inhabitants of outer space. All three teams must play in a game. The number on each team and the total number of players can change for each game.

Find the number of Yodos, Modos, and Hodos in each game.

1. There are 2 Yodos in a game.
   There are twice as many Hodos as Yodos.
   There are 55 players in all.

2. There are 48 Modos in another game.
   There are 12 fewer Hodos than Modos.
   There are 102 players in all.

3. There are 8 Modos in another game. There are 3 times as many Hodos as Modos. There are 60 players in all.

4. There are 12 Yodos in another game.
There are twice as many Modos as Hodos.
There are 60 players in all.

5. There are 30 Modos in another game.
There are half as many Hodos as Yodos.
There are 78 players in all.

ON YOUR OWN

Find the number of Yodos, Modos, and Hodos in each game.

1. There are 20 Hodos.
There are 8 fewer Modos than Hodos.
There are 82 players in all.

2. There are 15 Yodos.
There are 10 more Hodos than Modos.
There are 75 players in all.

3. There are 35 Modos.
There are twice as many Yodos as Hodos.
There are 80 players in all.

4. Make up a problem about 50 Yodos, Modos, and Hodos in a game. Trade problems with a classmate and solve.

5. *My Journal:* Which problem about Yodos, Modos, and Hodos was easiest for you to solve? Why? Which problem about Yodos, Modos, and Hodos was the most difficult for you to solve? Why?

Using Operations

▶ You need to buy 26 tickets for a baseball game. You have $348 and must spend it all. How many of each type of ticket can you buy?

▶ Suppose you had $348 to buy 26 tickets. This time you can spend all the money on tickets or save part of it to use for another activity. What combination(s) of back and front seats could you buy that would cost less than $348? How can you save the most money?

BaseBall GaME

fRONt $18
Back $12

Back
fRONt

Eight-Year-Old CARL

Have you ever wondered how people developed efficient ways to work with numbers? Carl Frederick Gauss was a German mathematician. When he was about eight years old, his teacher asked the class to find the sum of all the whole numbers from 1 to 100. It seemed like a task that would take a long time. Within seconds, Carl had the answer.

He used mental math strategies and multiplication. First he recognized that pairing the numbers would help.

Although we do not know their names, people in other parts of the world developed efficient systems, too. The people of Nigeria used Yoruba numbers for large quantities. The Yoruba system had 14 numbers: 1 to 10, 20, 30, 200, and 400. All other numbers were formed by adding, subtracting, or multiplying.

$$11 = 10 + 1 \qquad 40 = 20 \times 2$$
$$15 = 20 - 5 \qquad 50 = (20 \times 3) - 10$$

1 2 ... 49 51 ... 98 99 100

He got 49 sums of 100 or $49 \times 100 = 4900$. Then he added 50 and 100, the numbers that were not paired. He got the total of 5050.

1 Use Carl's method. Calculate the sum of all the numbers from 1 to 9. Then do the sum the long way. Do you get the same number?

2 Calculate the sum of all the numbers from 1 to 500.

3 Represent 28 and 42 in the Yoruba system.

Using Operations

▶ What is the total length of this cricket's jumps?

5 units   5 units   5 units   2 units   2 units   2 units   2 units

Jump Rules

In each problem, big jumps are the same length and little jumps are the same length. Jumps in different problems may be different lengths. Big jumps are longer than little jumps, and all jumps are a whole number of units long.

▶ How long is each jump?

1. Total length: 61 units

2. Total length: 24 units

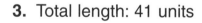

3. Total length: 41 units

4. Total length: 26 units

5. Total length: 28 units

▶ Solve these problems.
Use the same rules as on page 84.

1. Total length: 22 units. How long is each little jump?

5 units   5 units   ?   ?   ?

2. Total length: 22 units. How long is each big jump?

?   ?   ?   2 units   2 units

3. Total length: 50 units. How long is each jump?

4. *My Journal:* Which of the problems on this page was easiest to solve? Why? Which problem was most difficult? Why?

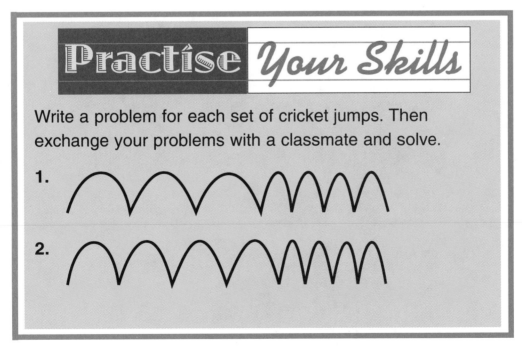

Practise Your Skills

Write a problem for each set of cricket jumps. Then exchange your problems with a classmate and solve.

1.

2.

FUN FUND RAISING!

What are some things you could do to raise money? Have you ever helped raise money by doing any of these kinds of activities? What project were you raising the money for?

Decide with your class what you would like to raise money for.

Car Wash
Cars $3.00

WIN A TV!

Raffle Tickets $2.00

TV Raffle

$2.00

Design a complete
plan for raising funds for
whatever your class decided on.
Then write a report describing
your plan and your work.
Here are some things
to think about.

- What should you consider when deciding how to raise funds?

- What expenses will you have?

- Will you sell tickets, a service, or an item?

- How much will you charge?

- How much money do you expect to raise?

- Is it possible that you could lose money? If so, how?

- How long will your fund-raising event last?

Check **Y**OURSELF

Great job! Your plan and report include all the important information about the fund-raising event. Your report explains clearly how you did your work. It shows an understanding of using appropriate operations and includes your personal strategies for them. Your plan and report were clear and easy to follow.

1. Use Carroll diagrams like these. Sort the numbers from 1 to 20.

	Composite Numbers	Prime Numbers
Even Numbers		
Odd Numbers		

	Prime Numbers	Composite Numbers
Factors of 12		
Not Factors of 12		

2. Use rectangular arrays to explain:
- why 7 is not a composite number, and
- why 24 is not a prime number.

3. Copy and complete the puzzle.

A **3**	B		C **4**	D
	E **3**	F		
G **6**		H **4**	I	
J	K **2**		L **1**	M
	N	**0**		

ACROSS

A: a multiple of 6

C: a multiple of 8

E: a multiple of 5

H: a multiple of 3

J: a multiple of 2

L: a multiple of 6

N: a multiple of 4

DOWN

B: a multiple of 7

D: a multiple of 9

F: a multiple of 6

G: a multiple of 8

I: a multiple of 7

K: a multiple of 11

M: a multiple of 8

4. Beth bought 16 packages of stickers. There were 24 stickers in each package. How many stickers did she get? She plans to put 8 stickers on each page of her sticker book. How many pages will her stickers fill?

5. Two hundred sixty-three children signed up for baseball. The coaches need help to figure out the number of teams of nine players they can make. Can you help them? Show how you solved the problem.

6. Elise has a 60-page photo album. She has used 12 pages already. She wants to use an equal number of the remaining pages for photos of each of her four brothers. How many pages will she have for photos of each brother? Show which operations you used.

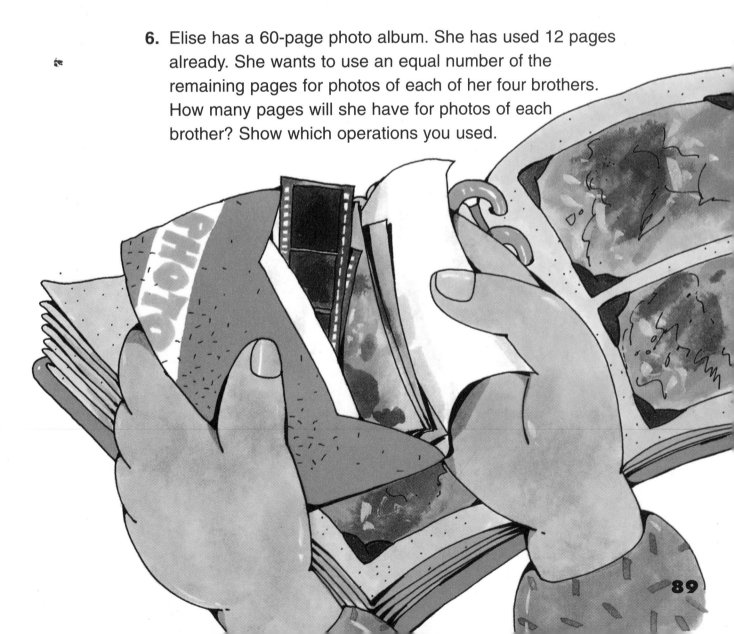

PROBLEM BANK

7. George Wedderburn, his 7-year-old sons Bret and Ben, and his 13-year-old daughter Tamika are planning to cruise the Thousand Islands.

Thousand Islands Day Cruise
All Rates Per Person
Children under 13 half-price when accompanied by an adult

	May and June	July and August	September
Reserved Deck Seats	$15.00	$25.00	$20.00
Reserved Inside Seats	$17.00	$15.00	$18.00
General Deck Seats	$10.00	$10.00	$10.00

a. Suppose the family reserved deck seats. How much more would it cost to travel in September than in June?

b. Use the Thousand Islands Cruise information. Write at least two problems that can be solved using different operations. Give your problems to a classmate to solve.

8. I am a number. Divide me by 10 and add 18. Then I am exactly what I started out as. What number am I?

9. I am a number. Add 3 times me to 4 and you get 10. What number am I?

10. Suppose you are at a movie with some friends. They give you their orders for popcorn and cola and the correct money. When you get to the refreshment counter, you forget how many popcorn and how many cola orders there were. You have $13.50. Popcorn is $3.00 and cola is $2.50. How many of each were ordered? Is there more than one possible answer?

11. Lester keeps a record of how far he jogs. Last week, from Monday to Friday, he jogged a total of 36 km. He knows he jogged 4 km on Monday, 8 km on Wednesday, 10 km on Friday, and that each day he jogged farther than the day before. How far did he jog on Tuesday and on Thursday?

12. We are two numbers. If you subtract one from the other you get 5. If you add us you get 35. What numbers are we?

13. We are two numbers. If you multiply our product by 2, you get 24. The difference between us is 1. What numbers are we?

14. We are two numbers. If you divide one of us by the other, you get 1 less than one of us. If you add us you get 25. What numbers are we?

SKILL
BANK
FROM THIS UNIT

1. Use the numbers in the box to find examples of these.
   a. a factor of 7
   b. a prime number
   c. a multiple of 3
   d. a composite number

7 13 18 20

2. Calculate.

a. 257 + 45	**b.** 87 + 69	**c.** 8276 + 951	**d.** 947 + 3882
e. 846 − 591	**f.** 470 − 88	**g.** 4962 − 46	**h.** 7306 − 428
i. 36 × 7	**j.** 8 × 39	**k.** 352 × 9	**l.** 5 × 444
m. 61 ÷ 7	**n.** 49 ÷ 4	**o.** 93 ÷ 5	**p.** 180 ÷ 3

3. Multiply.

a. 6 × 4	**b.** 8 × 400	**c.** 30 × 30	**d.** 40 × 60
6 × 70	8 × 20	30 × 7	40 × 5
6 × 74	8 × 5	4 × 7	9 × 60
	8 × 425	4 × 30	9 × 5
		34 × 37	49 × 65

4. Estimate. Then find the product.

a. 62 × 64	**b.** 18 × 55	**c.** 239 × 43	**d.** 47 × 46
e. 51 × 49	**f.** 435 × 78	**g.** 20 × 38	**h.** 393 × 65
i. 134 × 5	**j.** 3 × 638	**k.** 927 × 4	**l.** 8 × 493

5. Estimate. Then find the quotient.

a. 675 ÷ 5	**b.** 276 ÷ 3	**c.** 288 ÷ 6	**d.** 315 ÷ 7
e. 51 ÷ 4	**f.** 78 ÷ 5	**g.** 66 ÷ 8	**h.** 93 ÷ 5
i. 495 ÷ 6	**j.** 369 ÷ 4	**k.** 987 ÷ 5	**l.** 405 ÷ 7

SKILL BANK
LOOKING BACK

1. Draw the next three figures. Write the number pattern.

a.
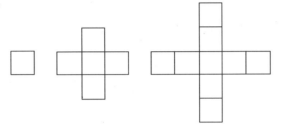

b.

2. Write the next three numbers in the pattern.

a. 600, 525, 450, 375, ■, ■, ■
b. 20, 25, 35, 50, 70, ■, ■, ■

3. What rules relates the first two numbers in each row to the third number?

a.

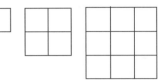

1	2	6
2	3	10
4	5	18
5	3	16

b.

3	3	7
6	1	4
5	5	23
4	4	14

4. Write the number in words.
a. 1001   **b.** 6060   **c.** 84 030
d. 20 200   **e.** 303 030   **f.** 570 002

5. Order the numbers from least to greatest.
a. 663, 360, 36 036, 330 600, 63 030
b. 100 100, 11 011, 10 101, 10 111, 10 010

6. Use the digits 8, 5, 1, 3, and 4.
a. Write the least number possible.
b. Write the greatest number possible.

93

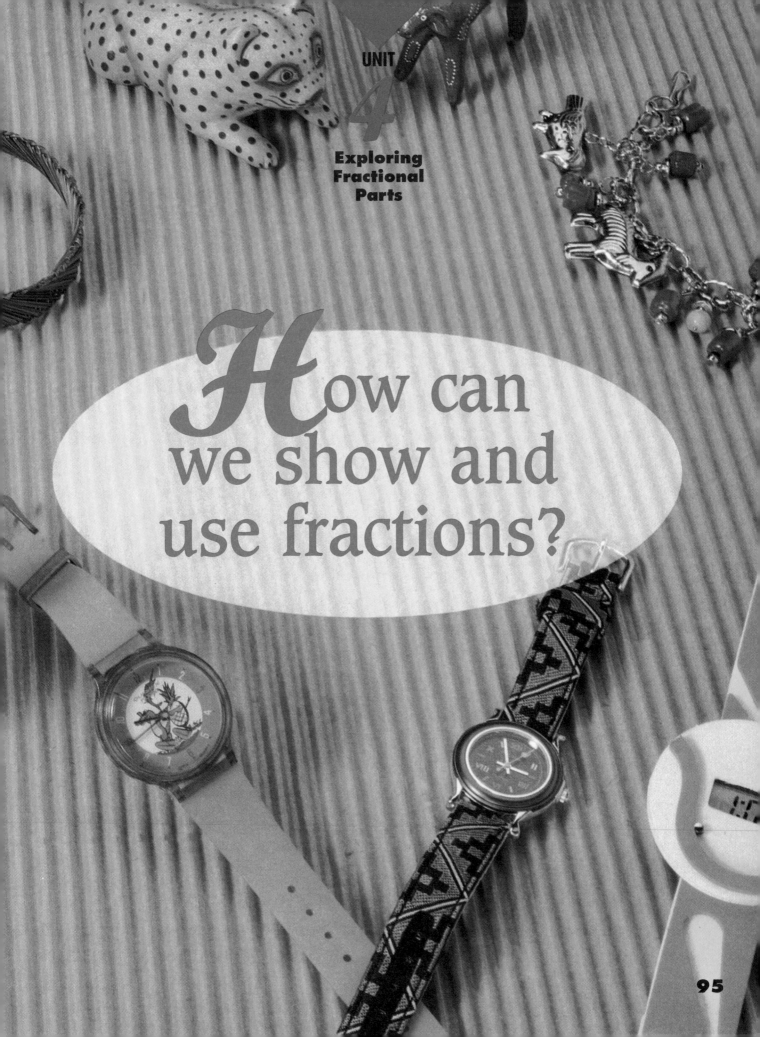

*H*ow can
we show and
use fractions?

EXPLORING FRACTIONAL PARTS

S·T·A·R·T·I·N·G OUT

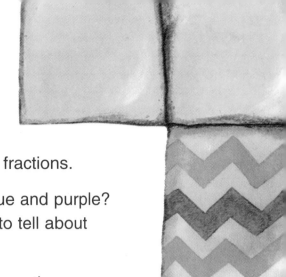

1 • Describe the quilt on page 96 using fractions.

• About what fraction of the quilt is blue and purple? What other fractions could you use to tell about the blue and purple squares?

• What colours in the quilt make up more than one quarter of it?

• Which colour in the quilt is more than one quarter but less than one half of it?

My Journal: What did you learn about comparing fractions from looking at the quilt?

2 • Which of these statements about this group do you think are true? Explain your thinking.

a. $\frac{10}{18}$ are girls.

b. About $\frac{1}{2}$ of the students are wearing solid colour shirts.

c. About $\frac{1}{3}$ of the students have brown hair and are wearing jeans.

d. $\frac{1}{6}$ of the students are not wearing striped shirts.

e. About $\frac{2}{3}$ of the students are wearing running shoes.

f. More than $\frac{3}{4}$ of the students are standing.

• What other statements about the group can you make using fractions?

• What statements using fractions can you make about the students in your class?

My Journal: What do you know about equivalent fractions from looking at this photograph and your class?

Exploring Parts of a Whole

▶ What fractions name the parts of each square?
What number sentences can you write for each
square?

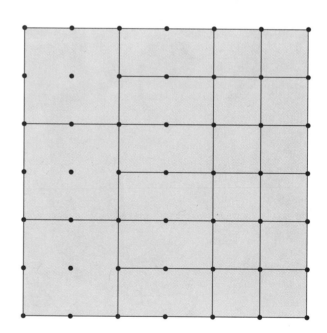

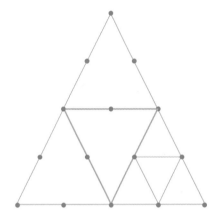

1. What fractions name the parts of this triangle? Explain how you know.

2. Suppose a circle is divided into these parts: $\frac{1}{4}$, $\frac{1}{8}$, $\frac{1}{8}$, and $\frac{1}{2}$. What could the circle look like? Sketch your idea and label the parts. Write a number sentence for the circle.

3. Draw a rectangle exactly like the one you see here. Divide it into parts so that you can describe the parts using at least 3 different fractions. Then try it again, dividing the rectangle into different parts.

4. *My Journal:* What have you learned about fractions that you did not know before? What questions do you have?

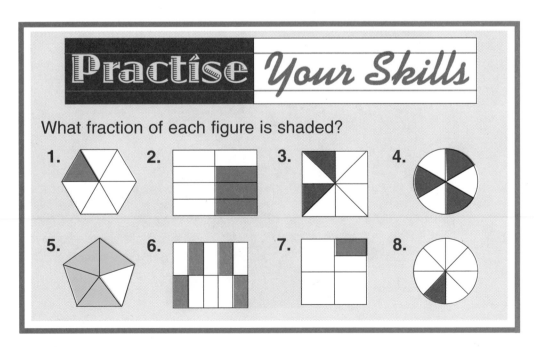

Practise Your Skills

What fraction of each figure is shaded?

1.
2.
3.
4.
5.
6.
7.
8.

Exploring Fractional Parts of a Set

▶ A party grab bag has some prizes in it.

Person 1 takes $\frac{1}{4}$ of the prizes, and passes the bag on to person 2.

Person 2 takes $\frac{1}{3}$ of the prizes that are left, and passes the bag on to person 3.

Person 3 takes $\frac{1}{2}$ of the prizes that are left, and passes the bag on to person 4.

There are 8 prizes left in the bag for person 4. How many prizes were in the grab bag to start with?

ON YOUR OWN

1. Plan a party. You have a box of 24 invitations. You will write 6 of the invitations. Three friends will share equally the writing of the remaining invitations. What fraction of the total number of invitations will each friend write?

2. You have enough money to buy 16 blueberry bagels to share with your guests. Each person gets the same number of bagels and there is no remainder. How many guests can you invite?

3. *My Journal:* Which was the most difficult problem to solve? Explain why.

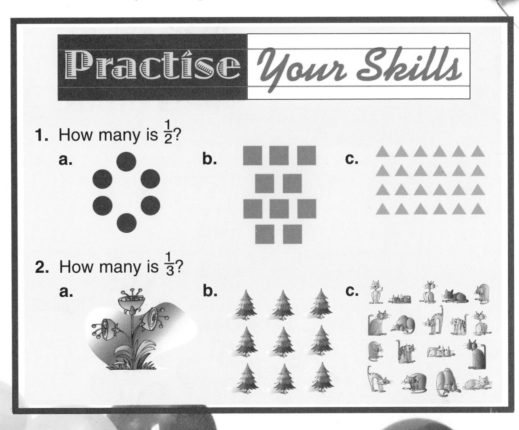

Practise Your Skills

1. How many is $\frac{1}{2}$?
   a.
   b.
   c.

2. How many is $\frac{1}{3}$?
   a.
   b.
   c.

Exploring Equivalent Fractions

▶ How many equivalent fractions can you find
using fraction circles?

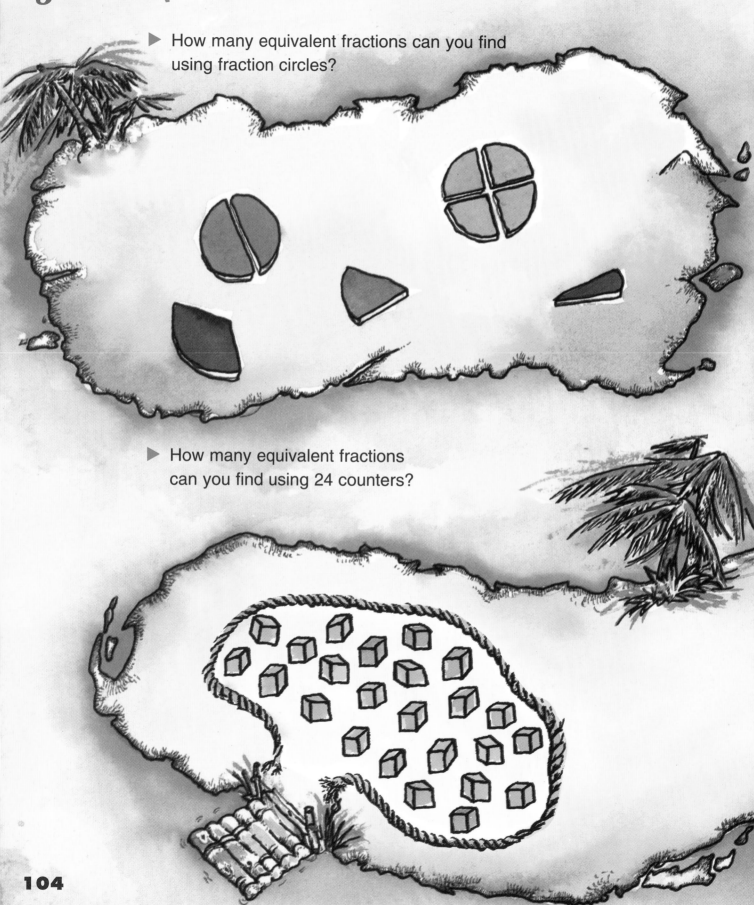

▶ How many equivalent fractions
can you find using 24 counters?

ON YOUR OWN

1. You receive a birthday cheque for $12.80. It is written with the fraction $\frac{80}{100}$. You know $\frac{80}{100}$ is not the simplest form of fraction. Should you ask the person who wrote the cheque to use the equivalent fraction $\frac{4}{5}$? Explain.

2. Is it always best to write fractions using the simplest form possible? Explain.

3. *My Journal:* What did you learn about fractions that was new? Explain.

Practise Your Skills

Copy and complete the equivalent fractions.

1. $\frac{1}{4} = \frac{\blacksquare}{8}$ $\frac{2}{4} = \frac{\blacksquare}{8}$ $\frac{3}{4} = \frac{\blacksquare}{8}$ $\frac{4}{4} = \frac{\blacksquare}{8}$

2. $\frac{1}{3} = \frac{\blacksquare}{6}$ $\frac{2}{3} = \frac{\blacksquare}{6}$ $\frac{3}{3} = \frac{\blacksquare}{6}$

3. $\frac{1}{5} = \frac{\blacksquare}{10}$ $\frac{2}{5} = \frac{\blacksquare}{10}$ $\frac{3}{5} = \frac{\blacksquare}{10}$ $\frac{4}{5} = \frac{\blacksquare}{10}$

Equivalent Fractions

▶ What's wrong with these pictures?

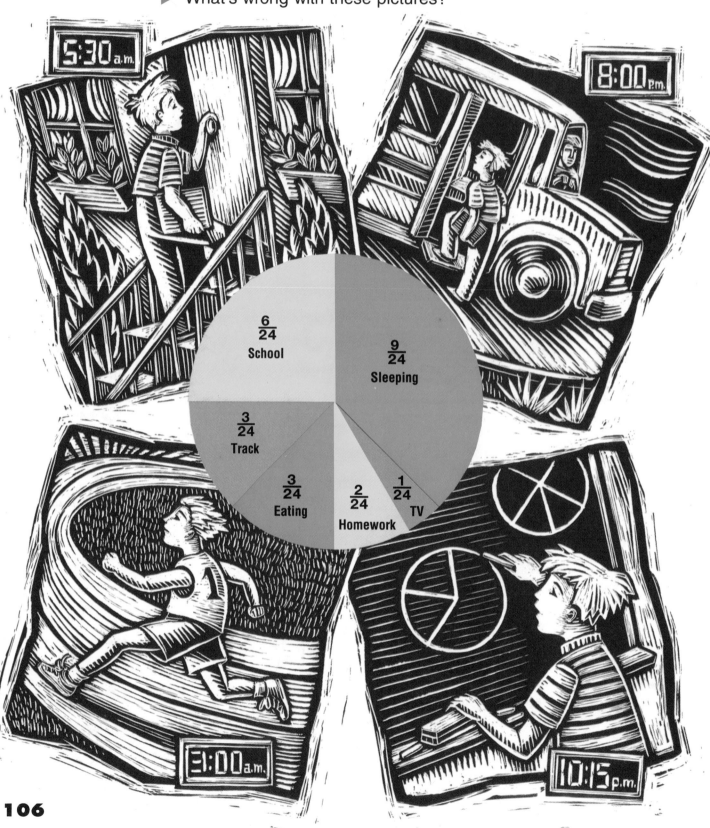

1. Make a circle graph. Show the typical day of a house pet, such as a cat, a dog, or a turtle.

2. Look at the pictures below. Write equivalent fractions for each situation.

3. Describe several different situations in which you would rather use a fraction that is not in simplest form. For each situation explain why you think it would be better to use a fraction that is not in simplest form.

4. *My Journal:* Is there anything about equivalent fractions that you still don't understand? Explain.

Fractions of TIME

Have you ever wondered how people who used other number systems expressed parts of one whole?

You know that you can express a part of a whole as a fraction or, in a base ten system, as a decimal. The Babylonians and the Alexandrians used a number system based on 60. The number 60 was useful because the year was considered to have 6 times 60 days.

The Greek astronomers developed their fraction system on the Babylonian base 60 system. The number 60 has many factors, so it was easy to represent parts of 60. Because 60 has factors of 2, 3, 4, 5, 6, 10, 12, 15, 20 and 30, fractions such as $\frac{1}{2}$, $\frac{1}{3}$, $\frac{1}{4}$, $\frac{1}{5}$, $\frac{1}{6}$, $\frac{1}{10}$, $\frac{1}{12}$, $\frac{1}{15}$, $\frac{1}{20}$, and $\frac{1}{30}$ were easily developed.

The notation for these fractions was, however, very different from the fraction notation used today.

1 What system based on 60 do you use every day?

2 What notation is used in our system for clock time? How would you represent $\frac{1}{2}$ hour? $\frac{1}{4}$ hour?

3 Draw a clock. Show $\frac{1}{2}$ hour, $\frac{1}{4}$ hour, $\frac{3}{4}$ hour and other fractional parts of an hour of your choice.

4 How does a digital clock show the times in exercise 3?

5 Explain how one clock can be used to show hours, minutes, and seconds.

6 Invent a system for showing parts of one whole.

# **M**easuring and Mixed Numbers

▶ Here's what you do.

1. Find some classroom objects to measure with your strip of paper.

2. Before you measure, estimate the lengths of the objects. Record, using fractions or mixed numbers.

3. Measure each object. Record your measurement using fractions or mixed numbers.

MEASURING CLASSROOM OBJECTS		
Object	**Estimate**	**Length**
Book	1 strip	$1\frac{3}{4}$ strips

DESCRIBING SPINNERS

with

FRACTIONS

How can you
describe these
spinners?
How do they
compare?
What type of
spinner do
you want
to make?
What will it
look like?

Make a spinner. Make sure that it has 8 equal parts. Colour it with 4 different colours. Before you start to use it, write about it. Use fractions to tell what it looks like. Predict how many times the spinner will land on each colour in 25 spins.

Spin the spinner 25 times. Describe the results using fractions that are related to the data. Then describe it using simpler fractions.

Spin the spinner 50 times. Use fractions to report on the data.

Compare the two sets of data. Use fractions as you tell how they compare.

Check YOURSELF

Great job! You created a spinner and described it using fractions. You predicted how the spinner would land. You used fractions to tell about your predictions. You collected and organized your data in a clear way. You wrote about your data using fractions and simpler, equivalent fractions. You ended your report with a comparison of the two sets of data.

PROBLEM BANK

1. Use coloured tiles. Make a rectangle that is $\frac{1}{2}$ red, $\frac{1}{5}$ blue, $\frac{1}{10}$ yellow, and $\frac{2}{10}$ green. Draw a picture of it and label it. What other rectangles can you draw to show the same fractions? Write some statements that compare the rectangles you have made.

2. You have a package of 48 jawbreakers. You grab a handful and find that you have 12. Then you give the rest to three friends to share equally. What fraction of the total package does each friend get? Will they agree that all of you got fair shares? Explain your thinking.

3. Your friend Kay has a pack of treats. She takes $\frac{1}{2}$ of the pack. She then passes the bag to Salim. He takes $\frac{1}{2}$ of the treats left. Then Tonya takes $\frac{1}{2}$ of what's left. That leaves 3 for you. How many treats were in Kay's bag to start with? How many did each person get? Explain how you know.

4. Here's a label on Salim's bag. He really doesn't want to share at all, so you'll never know what's inside. Use the label to decide what might be in the bag. Show some possibilities.

5. Make a bag of treats using small cubes to represent them. Find how many are in it. Write a label using fractions to tell about the different treats in it.

6. Draw 24 circles. Colour $\frac{1}{4}$ of them red, $\frac{1}{3}$ of them blue, and $\frac{2}{8}$ of them yellow. What fraction of the circles are not coloured?

7. Draw a rectangle. Colour about $\frac{2}{3}$ of it red. What other fractions can you use to tell about the coloured part? What fractions can you use to tell about the uncoloured part?

8. Alexis says she doesn't care whether she has $\frac{3}{4}$ or $\frac{7}{8}$ of a chocolate bar because either way a piece is missing. What would you say to help her better understand fractions? What pictures would you draw to help explain your ideas?

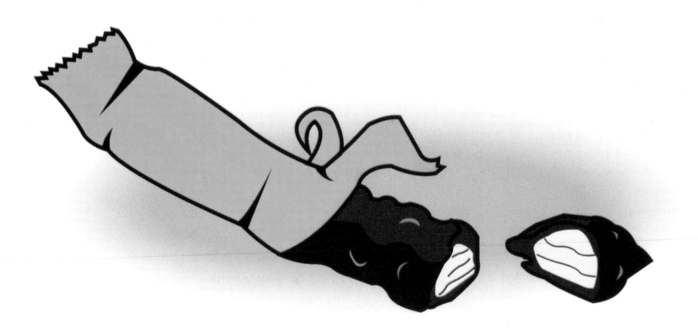

9. The grade five students are deciding where to go for their final trip. Here are the data they collected in the first survey.

Water slide	Overnight campout	Museum	National Park
	X		
	X		
	X		
	X		
X	X		
X	X		X
X	X		X
X	X	X	X
X	X	X	X
X	X	X	X
X	X	X	X

a. How can you use fractions to describe the data?

b. Is it true that more than $\frac{3}{4}$ don't want to go to the water slide?

c. Would $\frac{1}{2}$ of the students be happy if camping was the choice?

d. On the next survey, the museum will be eliminated as a choice. Those 4 students have to choose again. Is it possible for $\frac{2}{3}$ of the students to choose one of the remaining choices? Explain your thinking.

114

10. How many equivalent fractions can you write to tell about each pizza? Record them.

a.

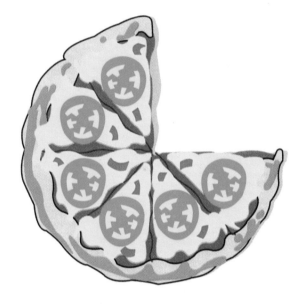

b.

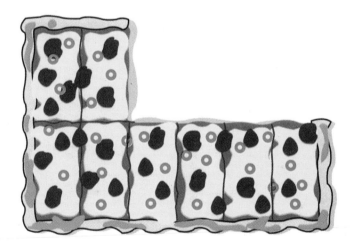

11. Eli used his strides to measure a room. He found it to be $8\frac{1}{2}$ strides long. Tess did the same thing. She found that it was $9\frac{3}{4}$ strides long. What do you know about Eli and Tess?

SKILL BANK
FROM THIS UNIT

1. Name the shaded fraction.

a.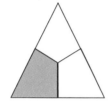

b.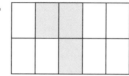

c.

2. How many is $\frac{1}{4}$?

3. How many is $\frac{2}{6}$?

4. How many is $\frac{2}{3}$?

5. How many is $\frac{3}{8}$?

6. Copy and complete the equivalent fractions.

a. $\frac{1}{3} = \frac{\blacksquare}{12}$ **b.** $\frac{1}{3} = \frac{\blacksquare}{9}$ **c.** $\frac{2}{3} = \frac{\blacksquare}{12}$ **d.** $\frac{2}{3} = \frac{\blacksquare}{9}$

e. $\frac{1}{4} = \frac{\blacksquare}{8}$ **f.** $\frac{1}{4} = \frac{\blacksquare}{16}$ **g.** $\frac{3}{4} = \frac{\blacksquare}{8}$ **h.** $\frac{2}{4} = \frac{\blacksquare}{16}$

i. $\frac{1}{5} = \frac{\blacksquare}{10}$ **j.** $\frac{1}{5} = \frac{\blacksquare}{25}$ **k.** $\frac{4}{5} = \frac{\blacksquare}{10}$ **l.** $\frac{3}{5} = \frac{\blacksquare}{25}$

7. Write the mixed number.

a.   **b.**   **c.**

SKILL BANK LOOKING BACK

1. Write the numeral for each.
   a. three hundred sixty thousand eighteen
   b. twenty thousand two
   c. nine hundred thousand
   d. 800 000 + 8000 + 80
   e. 90 000 + 90 + 9

2. Use the numbers in the box.
   a. Which number is closest to 86 400?
   b. Which number is 500 greater than 86 400?
   c. Which number is 1 more than 86 999?
   d. Which number is 500 less than 87 900?

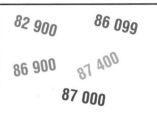

82 900   86 099

86 900   87 400

87 000

3. a. Name three prime numbers between 10 and 18.
   b. Is 4 a composite number? Explain why or why not.
   c. Name all the factors of 9.

4. Calculate.
   a. 7894 + 507   b. 84 + 9098   c. 563 + 3792
   d. 602 − 487   e. 4913 − 1587   f. 9002 − 1545

5. Estimate. Then find the product.
   a. 57 × 84   b. 529 × 44   c. 728 × 3   d. 691 × 5
   e. 183 × 77   f. 93 × 56   g. 47 × 65   h. 7 × 378

6. Estimate. Then find the quotient
   a. 320 ÷ 5   b. 627 ÷ 3   c. 208 ÷ 6   d. 501 ÷ 8
   e. 98 ÷ 4   f. 85 ÷ 2   g. 77 ÷ 6   h. 61 ÷ 9

How can we show and use decimals?

Hundred Chart

1	2	3	4	5	6	7	8	9	10
11	12	13	14	15	16	17	18	19	20
21	22	23	24	25	26	27	28	29	30
31	32	33	34	35	36	37	38	39	40
41	42	43	44	45	46	47	48	49	50
51	52	53	54	55	56	57	58	59	60
61	62	63	64	65	66	67	68	69	70
71	72	73	74	75	76	77	78	79	80
81	82	83	84	85	86	87	88	89	90
91	92	93	94	95	96	97	98	99	100

1. • What fraction of the numbers on the chart are less than 51? How can you express that in another way?

   • What fraction of the numbers have a two in the tens place? What other fractions can you use to express the answer?

   • What fraction of the numbers on the chart are in one row of the chart?

   • Express all your fraction answers as decimals.

   • Write your own question about the hundred chart. Challenge a partner to answer it using fractions and decimals.

My Journal: When do you think fractions and decimals are useful? Describe a situation in which you think it is better to use one rather than the other.

**BUILDING RATIONAL
NUMBER SENSE**

**S·T·A·R·T·I·N·G
OUT**

2 ● At the 1992 Olympic Summer Games, these were the results of one women's rowing event:

● Final Results

China: 6 minutes 32.50 seconds
Germany: 6 minutes 32.34 seconds
Canada: 6 minutes 30.85 seconds
Australia: 6 minutes 41.72 seconds
United States: 6 minutes 31.86 seconds
Romania: 6 minutes 37.24 seconds

● Which team came first? second? sixth?

● Use decimals to describe what a last-place finish could have been.

● Use decimals to describe the difference between the times of the first-place team and the sixth-place team.

● Use decimals to describe a time the fourth-place team would have needed to win the bronze medal.

My Journal: What questions do you have about ordering decimals? How would you explain to a partner some rules for ordering decimals?

Representing Decimal Numbers

▶ How can you show the decimals below on a number line?

73% LESS FAT THAN OATMEAL!

HOT CEREAL

Original

336 g

12 single serving packets

Nutritional Information

per 28 g serving

Protein	3.4 g
Fat	0.43 g
Polyunsaturates	0.30 g
Monounsaturates	0.05 g
Saturates	0.08 g
Cholesterol	0.0 mg
Carbohydrates	20.9 g
Sugars	6.2 g
Starch	13.4 g
Dietary Fibre	1.3 g

1. Write the decimal for each letter.

a.
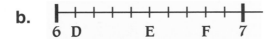
A   1   B   C 2

b.
6 D   E   F 7

c.
123 G   H   124   I   125

2. Trace each part of a number line on your paper. Estimate to locate the decimal.

a. Label 1.75.

0 0.25

b. Label 3.

0   0.5

3. *My Journal:* What do you know about how decimals are related to fractions?

Practise Your Skills

Write each fraction as a decimal.

1. $\frac{1}{10}$ **2.** $\frac{8}{10}$ **3.** $\frac{8}{100}$ **4.** $\frac{80}{100}$

5. $\frac{2}{4}$ **6.** $\frac{3}{5}$ **7.** $\frac{1}{5}$ **8.** $\frac{3}{6}$

9. five tenths   **10.** nine tenths

11. seven hundredths   **12.** seventy hundredths

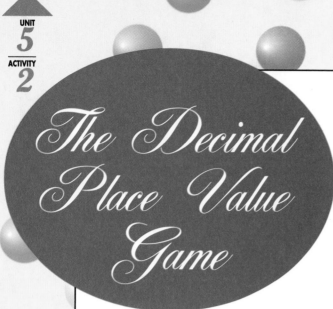

The Decimal Place Value Game

Group

2 players

Materials

- a game board for each player

___ ___ • ___ ___ ___

- number cards, 0–9
- score sheet

Game Rules

Game 1
Goal: Build a decimal closer to 1.

Each player makes a game board as shown. Each pair makes a score sheet.

1 One player shuffles the number cards, then places them face down on the table.

2 The other player takes the top card and places it on one of the empty spaces on her or his game board. Once a card is down, it cannot be moved.

3 Players have turns taking and placing cards until each player has had three turns. Players read and compare the decimals they have made. The player who makes a decimal closer to 1 scores a point.

4 Players continue playing for five rounds, taking turns shuffling the cards and starting each round.

Game 2
Goal: Make the lesser number.

Follow the rules for Game 1 with this new goal.

Game 3
Goal: Make the greater number.

Follow the rules for Game 1 with this new goal.

Example: Game 3

	David	Lien
Turn 1	_ . 3 _	_ . 8 _
Turn 2	2 . 3 _	_ . 8 7
Turn 3	2 . 3 9	5 . 8 7

Who won?

ON YOUR OWN

Here is one way to vary The Decimal Place Value Game. Switch the places of any two cards after three cards have been placed on the game board.

1. Suppose you made the decimal 1.29. What numbers greater than 1.29 can you make by switching two digits?

2. Suppose you made the decimal 3.40. What numbers less than 3.40 can you make by switching two digits?

3. *My Journal:* How do you know when one decimal is greater than another? Use examples in your explanation.

Practise Your Skills

Copy and write > (greater than) or < (less than) for each ■.

1. 7.5 ■ 8.3 **2.** 9.7 ■ 8.9 **3.** 6.81 ■ 6.71

4. 9.60 ■ 9.07 **5.** 16.5 ■ 16.4 **6.** 0.80 ■ 0.75

List each set of numbers from least to greatest.

7. 3.96, 3.69, 3.71 **8.** 57.0, 57.2, 56.9 **9.** 17.03, 17.30, 18.10

Adding and Subtracting Decimals

▶ What lunches could you order from this menu for $7.50 or less? Find as many different possibilities as you can.

ZEBRA DINER!

SOUPS AND SALADS

tomato soup —— 1.95
black bean soup —— 2.25
taco salad —— 3.25
tuna salad —— 2.95
chef's Salad —— 3.99
small green salad — 1.75

SANDWICHES

turkey —— 4.35
ham and cheese — 5.95
bean burrito —— 2.99
chicken burrito — 3.59
hamburger —— 3.79
cheeseburger —— 9.39
grilled chicken — 4.75

HOT DISHES

beef chili —— 5.95
macaroni and cheese — 4.59
chimichanga —— 5.75
franks and beans —— 3.89
veal parmigiana —— 5.95

BEVERAGES AND DESSERTS

Pie —— 1.95
fruit salad —— 1.49
ice cream sundae —— 3.59
milk/chocolate milk — 1.25
juices —— 1.45

Use the menu on page 128.

ON YOUR OWN

1. Suppose you were allergic to dairy products. Which items would you order for lunch? What is the total cost of those items?

2. Suppose you were a vegetarian. Which items would you order for lunch? What is the total cost of those items?

3. Suppose you were treating a friend to lunch. You had $15. What would the two of you order? What is the total cost of your lunch?

4. *My Journal:* What have you learned about adding and subtracting decimals?

Practise Your Skills

Add.

1. 4.59 + 0.89   2. 63.8 + 1.79   3. 6.4 + 0.5

4. 8.9 + 7.8   5. 1.54 + 3.63   6. 26.2 + 5.7

Subtract.

7. 17.4 − 6.7   8. 27.9 − 19.6   9. 26.26 − 18.94

10. 8.7 − 3.9   11. 76.3 − 20.5   12. 86.52 − 59.2

Solving Problems with Money

▶ Estimate first, then solve the problems.

1. Suppose you have $1.50 to spend on pretzels. You spend all of your money. How many pretzels can you get?

**Soft pretzels
$0.25 each.
Buy 3 get
1 free.**

2. Buy a battery. Use ten coins. What coins will you use?

**Batteries
$0.73 each**

3. You have $3.70 in dimes and quarters. You have nine more dimes than quarters. How many quarters do you have?

4. Suppose you were asked to shovel snow every day it snowed one winter. You agreed on a pay of $0.01 for the first day, $0.02 for the second day, $0.04 the third day, $0.08 on the fourth day, and so on. You work thirteen days that winter. How much will you be paid on the thirteenth day? How much will you be paid altogether?

5. You have $52 to buy tickets for the community play. Adult tickets are $7.50 each. Student tickets are $4.75 each. You buy eight tickets and get $0.25 change. How many of each kind of ticket did you buy?

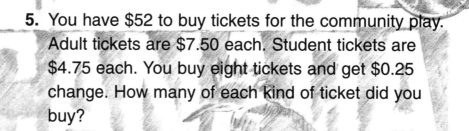

ON YOUR OWN

Refer to the problems on page 130.

1. Read problem 1 to answer these questions.

   a. How much would it cost to get two pretzels? five pretzels?
   b. What plan can you follow to find the cost of any number of pretzels?

2. Read problem 2 to answer these questions.

   a. Suppose you paid with 17 coins. What coins would you use to buy the battery?
   b. What is the least number of coins you could use to buy the battery?

3. Read problem 5 to answer this question.

   Suppose you had $25.00 and bought at least one of each kind of ticket. How many of each kind could you buy?

4. *My Journal:* Which problem did you enjoy the most? Why? What strategies did you use to solve it?

Practise Your Skills

Add.

1. 5.6 + 9.2 + 6.1

2. 9.8 + 9.7 + 10.0

3. 8.4 + 12.5 + 61.8

4. 69.8 + 50.6 + 29

5. 28.09 + 9.99 + 68.51

6. 2.00 + 1.68 + 2.37

Write each money amount using decimals.

7. seven quarters

8. twelve dimes

9. eighteen nickels

Measuring the World

Have you ever wondered why the metric system was created? Before it came into being, people in certain regions had their own standard measures. But in other regions, those measures did not mean the same thing. Can you imagine trying to build homes, plant fields, or measure clothes, if everybody had a different idea of what each measure was?

In the late 1700s, the French decided to create a measure based on Earth. They took the length of the meridian (an imaginary line that circles Earth between the North Pole and the South Pole) and divided it by 40 000 000. That length became the metre. Many measurements in the metric system can be calculated by dividing or multiplying the metre by 10, 100, 1000, 10 000, or a subsequent number in this pattern.

1. How do you use decimals to show metric measures? Write decimals to show how 1 cm, 10 cm, and 1 dm are part of a metre.

2. Why do you think using the metric system makes sense?

3. Explain any patterns you see in the metric system.

Estimate and Solve

▶ For each problem, estimate the solution. Then find a solution using any method you can.

1. A battery for a lap-top computer is advertised as a long-life battery. Suppose a typical battery lasts about 90 minutes. About how long might you expect a long-life battery to last?

2. **A store sold** an estimated 6600 cans and bottles of soft drinks one month. The graph shows what part of this number was sold in each type of container. About how many of each type were sold?

NEW LONG-LIFE
BATTERY
FOR LAPTOPS

We guarantee
1.5 times the
running time!
Try us and see!
Call 555-LONG

PACKAGING OF SOFT DRINKS

0.75
plastic bottles

0.11

0.14

355-mL cans

glass bottles

3. What is the mean price of these compact discs?

$17.99

$24.98

$19.49

4. Find the price
of one doughnut,
one cookie,
one muffin,
and one bun.

STAR BAKERY

DOUGHNUTS
$2.75/
HALF DOZEN

COOKIES
3 FOR $0.89

MUFFINS
6 FOR $3.50

BUNS
8 FOR $2.00

ON YOUR OWN

Estimate. Then find the solution to each problem.

1. Trish swims 2.4 km a day, five days a week.
How far does she swim in a week?

2. Mitchell swam 13.5 km in five days.
On average, how far did he swim each day?

3. Laryssa phoned home after a swim meet. She talked for 3 minutes
when the rate was $0.40 per minute. How much did her call cost?

4. Jerod also phoned home after the swim meet. He talked for 7 minutes.
His phone bill was $3.15. What was the cost per minute for Jerod's
call?

134

5. Try to cover four squares in a row, column, or diagonal on this game board.

- Choose one factor from each group.
- Find the product using any method.
- Cover the product in a square with a counter or penny.
- Continue choosing pairs of factors until you have covered four squares in a row.

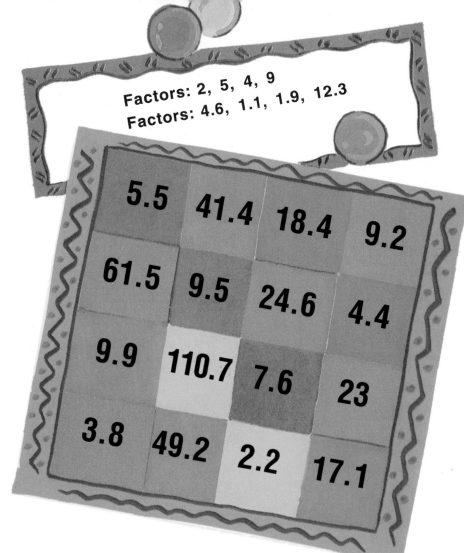

Factors: 2, 5, 4, 9
Factors: 4.6, 1.1, 1.9, 12.3

5.5	41.4	18.4	9.2
61.5	9.5	24.6	4.4
9.9	110.7	7.6	23
3.8	49.2	2.2	17.1

6. *My Journal:* What have you learned about multiplying and dividing decimals?

Practise Your Skills

Multiply.

1. 12.1 x 5   **2.** 361.3 x 7   **3.** 110.8 x 4   **4.** 67.6 x 2

5. 3 x 543.6   **6.** 8 x 16.53   **7.** 6 x 43.65   **8.** 9 x 209.9

Divide.

9. 16.2 ÷ 3   **10.** 11.2 ÷ 7   **11.** 22.8 ÷ 4   **12.** 2.8 ÷ 5

13. 0.21 ÷ 3   **14.** 33.3 ÷ 9   **15.** 50.64 ÷ 6   **16.** 75.6 ÷ 9

The Missing Factor Game

Group

4 players

Materials

- a list of factors and product ranges for each round

Round	Factor	Product Range
1	15.4	between 150 and 200
2	18.2	between 60 and 90
3	23.2	between 200 and 250
4	62	between 20 and 40
5	89	between 50 and 70
6	32.5	between 250 and 300

- recording sheet

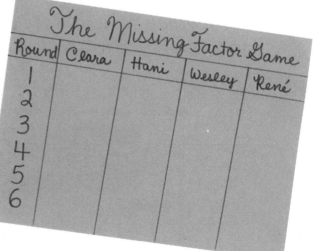

- a calculator for each player

Game Rules

1. Each player looks at the factor for Round 1. He or she uses mental math or estimation to select a number that can be multiplied by that factor to get a product within the range shown.

2. Each player multiplies the number he or she selected by the given factor using a calculator. If the product is within the given range, the player writes the multiplication sentence on the recording sheet.

3. Students compare multiplication sentences.

4. Play continues for five more rounds.

5. Players make up a list of six factors and product ranges for a new game.

137

The Effect of a Surface on Ball Bounce Height

When you drop a ball, it rises to a certain height on the first bounce. What factors might cause this "bounce height" to change?

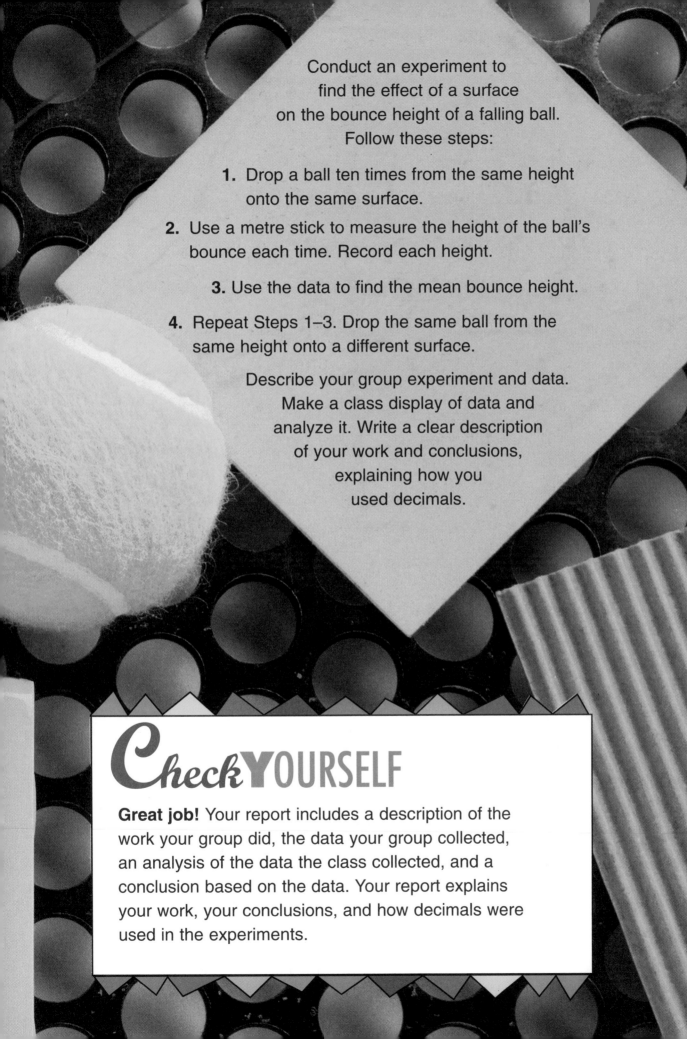

Conduct an experiment to
find the effect of a surface
on the bounce height of a falling ball.
Follow these steps:

1. Drop a ball ten times from the same height
   onto the same surface.

2. Use a metre stick to measure the height of the ball's
   bounce each time. Record each height.

3. Use the data to find the mean bounce height.

4. Repeat Steps 1–3. Drop the same ball from the
   same height onto a different surface.

Describe your group experiment and data.
Make a class display of data and
analyze it. Write a clear description
of your work and conclusions,
explaining how you
used decimals.

*Check*YOURSELF

Great job! Your report includes a description of the
work your group did, the data your group collected,
an analysis of the data the class collected, and a
conclusion based on the data. Your report explains
your work, your conclusions, and how decimals were
used in the experiments.

PROBLEM BANK

1. Draw circles like these. Sort all the decimals into the circles.

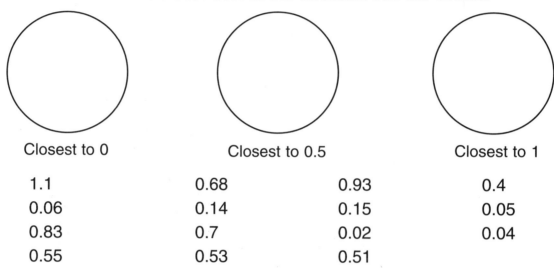

Closest to 0	Closest to 0.5		Closest to 1
1.1	0.68	0.93	0.4
0.06	0.14	0.15	0.05
0.83	0.7	0.02	0.04
0.55	0.53	0.51	

2. Name at least 3 decimals between each pair.
   a. 0.5 and 1.0
   b. 0.25 and 0.75
   c. 0 and 0.1
   d. 0.87 and 1

3. Use the number started in the box on the right.
   Fill in the spaces to make these numbers.
   a. a number between 60 and 70
   b. the greatest possible number
   c. the least possible number
   d. a number close to 74
   e. a number close to 31

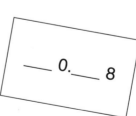

___ 0.___ 8

4.

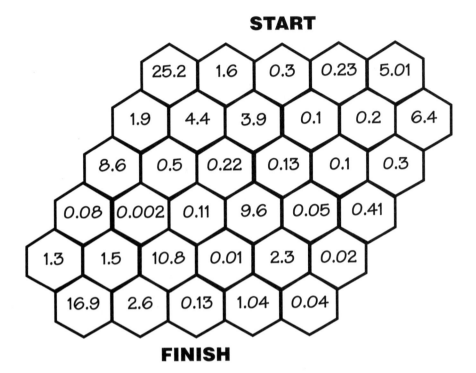

START

25.2	1.6	0.3	0.23	5.01
1.9	4.4	3.9	0.1	0.2	6.4
8.6	0.5	0.22	0.13	0.1	0.3
0.08	0.002	0.11	9.6	0.05	0.41
1.3	1.5	10.8	0.01	2.3	0.02
16.9	2.6	0.13	1.04	0.04

FINISH

a. Find a path through the maze. Use only one cell from each row. The sum of all the decimals along your path must be the greatest possible number. Write the number and your path as you follow it.

b. Try to find a path that leads to a finish number of exactly 1. What path did you find?

c. Try to find a path that leads to a finish number that is as close as possible to 50. What path did you find?

d. Try to find a path that leads to the least possible finish number. What path did you find?

PROBLEM BANK

5. a. Choose three items from the flyer. What is the total cost?

b. Choose two items from the flyer. How much money would you have left from $20.00?

c. Make up some more problems about the flyer for someone else to solve.

6. There are 3.9 g of protein in each 40-g serving of Fruit and Fibre cereal. Approximately how many grams of protein are there in a 425-g box?

7. Write a story problem for each expression. Then solve the problems.

a. 9.6 – 1.64
b. 8 x 1.57
c. 62.4 + 937.62
d. $8.95 ÷ 4

8. Estimate, then use any method to find the solutions.

a. One pair of sandals costs $3.29. Can you buy six pairs with $19.00? Explain.

b. Gasoline costs 54.6 cents per litre. How much will 45 L cost?

9. Without calculating, tell everything you know about the solution to each expression and how you know it.

    a. 1.86 + 2.45

    b. 2.32 x 6

    c. 7.6 ÷ 2

    d. 93.2 − 0.06

    e. 25.1 x 3

    f. 89.4 ÷ 10

10. Find the missing factor in each problem. Use your calculator and the "guess-and-check" problem-solving strategy. Record all your guesses.

    a. 50 x ■ is between 85 and 95.

    b. 14 x ■ is between 57 and 66.

    c. 6 x ■ is between 90 and 110.

11. Estimate whether each expression will have a product that is less than or greater than 400. Explain your reasoning.

    a. 37.9 x 5

    b. 45.4 x 9

    c. 81.1 x 7

    d. 21.6 x 5

    e. 28.4 x 8

    f. 84.5 x 9

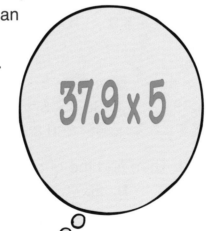

1. Write each as a decimal number.

a. $\frac{1}{10}$　　**b.** $\frac{3}{10}$　　**c.** $\frac{3}{100}$　　**d.** $\frac{31}{100}$

e. $\frac{1}{4}$　　**f.** $\frac{1}{5}$　　**g.** $\frac{3}{4}$　　**h.** $\frac{3}{5}$

i. two tenths　　　**j.** nine tenths　　　**k.** five hundredths

2. Copy each expression. Instead of ■, write < or >.

a. 7.7 ■ 6.6　　　　**b.** 0.9 ■ 9.0　　　　**c.** 14.6 ■ 41.2

d. 8.47 ■ 8.74　　　**e.** 9.35 ■ 9.32　　　**f.** 46.19 ■ 43.97

3. Order the numbers from least to greatest.

a. 5.82, 8.52, 2.58, 5.28　　　　**b.** 37.09, 39.3, 37.03, 39.07

4. Add.

a. 8.19 + 1.06　　　**b.** 73.2 + 10.4　　　**c.** 6.43 + 5.28

d. 7.3 + 4.5　　　　**e.** 3.4 + 8.15　　　　**f.** 7.52 + 7.6

g. 4.7 + 6.1 + 5.9　　**h.** 32.6 + 47.8 + 23.5

5. Multiply.

a. 7.2 × 4　　**b.** 4.89 × 5　　**c.** 9.2 × 3　　**d.** 5 × 9.63

e. 5 × 89.2　　**f.** 33.6 × 8　　**g.** 12.16 × 8　　**h.** 7 × 54.9

i. 163.4 × 6　　**j.** 4 × 560.8　　**k.** 231.7 × 9　　**l.** 2 × 547.3

6. Estimate. Then find the quotient.

a. 75.5 ÷ 5　　**b.** 26.48 ÷ 4　　**c.** 49.2 ÷ 6　　**d.** 32.9 ÷ 7

e. 0.69 ÷ 3　　**f.** 97.6 ÷ 8　　**g.** 76.02 ÷ 6　　**h.** 40.5 ÷ 5

7. Find a factor so that the product is in the given range.

a. 12.5 × ■ = a product between 60 and 70

b. 6 × ■ = a product between 36 and 40

c. 79 × ■ = a product between 140 and 180

S K I L L BANK
LOOKING BACK

1. **a.** Name the factors of 8.
   b. Name four multiples of 3.
   c. Is 5 a prime number? Explain why or why not.
   d. Which of these numbers are composite numbers?
   10, 11, 12, 13, 14, 15

2. Estimate. Then find the product.
   a. 62×25 **b.** 231×56 **c.** 487×6 **d.** 7×936
   e. 39×432 **f.** 18×18 **g.** 8×109 **h.** 9×345

3. Estimate. Then find the quotient.
   a. $485 \div 5$ **b.** $350 \div 20$ **c.** $672 \div 6$ **d.** $297 \div 9$
   e. $46 \div 3$ **f.** $69 \div 4$ **g.** $90 \div 6$ **h.** $72 \div 7$

4. What part of the set in the box is this?
   a. $\frac{1}{2}$ **b.** $\frac{1}{3}$ **c.** $\frac{1}{4}$
   d. $\frac{1}{8}$ **e.** $\frac{1}{6}$ **f.** $\frac{2}{3}$
   g. $\frac{3}{4}$ **h.** $\frac{5}{6}$ **i.** $\frac{3}{8}$

5. Copy and complete the equivalent fractions.
   a. $\frac{1}{3} = \frac{\blacksquare}{15}$ **b.** $\frac{2}{3} = \frac{\blacksquare}{15}$ **c.** $\frac{1}{6} = \frac{\blacksquare}{18}$ **d.** $\frac{4}{6} = \frac{\blacksquare}{18}$
   e. $\frac{1}{5} = \frac{\blacksquare}{20}$ **f.** $\frac{2}{5} = \frac{\blacksquare}{20}$ **g.** $\frac{1}{10} = \frac{\blacksquare}{40}$ **h.** $\frac{7}{10} = \frac{\blacksquare}{40}$

6. Write the mixed number.
   a.    **b.**    **c.**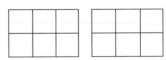

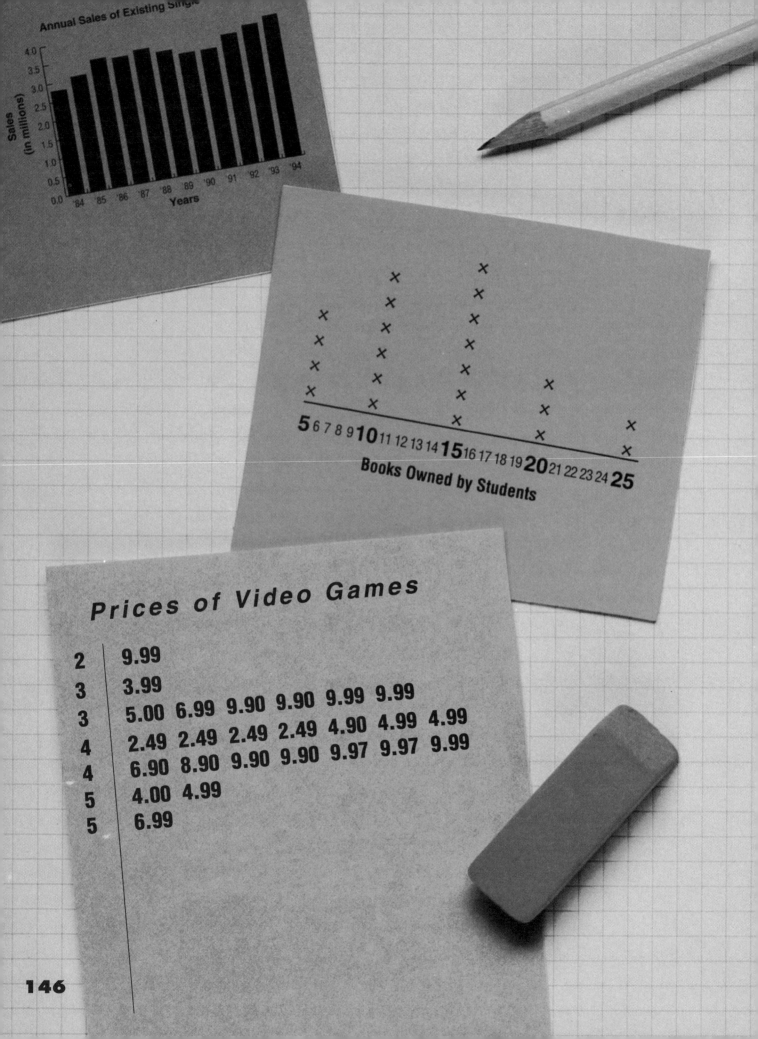

Annual Sales of Existing Single

Books Owned by Students

5 6 7 8 9 **10** 11 12 13 14 **15** 16 17 18 19 **20** 21 22 23 24 **25**

Prices of Video Games

2	9.99
3	3.99
3	5.00 6.99 9.90 9.90 9.99 9.99
4	2.49 2.49 2.49 2.49 4.90 4.99 4.99
4	6.90 8.90 9.90 9.90 9.97 9.97 9.99
5	4.00 4.99
5	6.99

NHL Teams That Have Gone
the Longest without Winning
Their Division (in years):

New York Rangers **47**

Chicago **40**

Toronto **31**

Los Angeles **23**

Pittsburgh **23**

*W*hat patterns can we see in data?

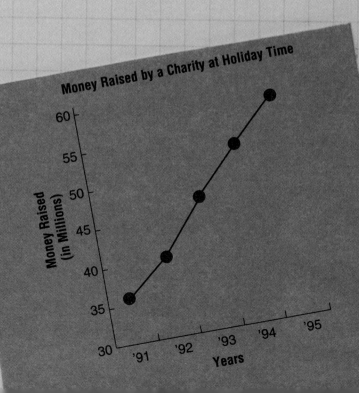

Money Raised by a Charity at Holiday Time

5	4 4 4 4
5	6 6 6 6
6	1 1 1 1 3
6	5 5 5 5
7	0 2
7	7 7 7 7 7
8	5

**Masses of High
School Wrestlers in
Kilograms**

147

COLLECTING AND
ANALYZING DATA

S·T·A·R·T·I·N·G
OUT

Best Batting Averages of All Time

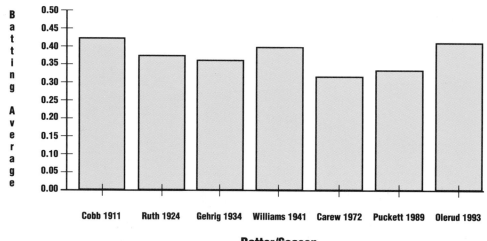

 **Batting Average**

How Melissa Spends Her Time On An Average School Day

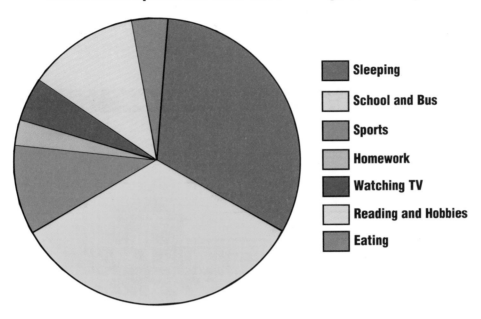

Sleeping
School and Bus
Sports
Homework
Watching TV
Reading and Hobbies
Eating

1 • What information can you learn from the bar graph?

• What other ways can you think of to show this information?

• What information can you learn from the circle graph?

• Estimate how much time Melissa spends playing sports. Is that more or less time than she spends watching TV? Explain how you know.

• On which activity does Melissa spend the most time?

• How else could you show the information about how Melissa spends her time?

My Journal: Why might you show information on a graph?

COLLECTING AND
ANALYZING DATA

Number of Books I Have Read

Name	Number of Books
Ahmed	⊕⊕⊕⊕⊕ ⊕⊕⊕⊕⊕
Bonnie	⊕⊕⊕⊕⊕ ⊕⊕⊕⊕⊕ ⊕⊕⊕⊕⊕ ⊕⊕⊕⊕⊕
Bryan	⊕⊕⊕⊕⊕ ⊕⊕⊕⊕⊕ ⊕⊕⊕
Charles	⊕⊕⊕⊕⊕ ⊕⊕⊕⊕⊕ ⊕⊕⊕⊕⊕
Cleon	⊕⊕⊕⊕⊕ ⊕⊕⊕⊕⊕ ⊕⊕⊕⊕⊕ ⊕⊕⊕⊕⊕
Cydney	⊕⊕⊕⊕⊕
Dana	⊕⊕⊕⊕⊕ ⊕⊕⊕⊕⊕ ⊕⊕⊕⊕⊕ ⊕⊕⊕⊕⊕ ⊕⊕⊕⊕⊕
Daniel	⊕⊕⊕⊕⊕ ⊕⊕⊕⊕⊕ ⊕⊕⊕⊕⊕ ⊕⊕⊕⊕⊕
Devon	⊕⊕⊕⊕⊕ ⊕⊕⊕⊕⊕ ⊕⊕⊕⊕⊕ ⊕⊕⊕⊕⊕
Farah	⊕⊕⊕⊕⊕ ⊕⊕⊕⊕⊕
Fatima	⊕⊕⊕⊕⊕ ⊕⊕⊕⊕⊕ ⊕⊕⊕⊕⊕ ⊕⊕⊕
Hsiao	⊕⊕⊕⊕⊕ ⊕⊕⊕⊕⊕ ⊕⊕⊕⊕⊕ ⊕⊕⊕⊕⊕ ⊕⊕⊕⊕⊕ ⊕
Jamie	⊕⊕⊕⊕⊕ ⊕⊕⊕
Janelle	⊕⊕⊕⊕⊕ ⊕⊕⊕⊕⊕ ⊕⊕⊕⊕⊕ ⊕⊕⊕⊕⊕ ⊕⊕⊕⊕⊕
Jordana	⊕⊕⊕⊕⊕ ⊕⊕⊕⊕⊕ ⊕⊕⊕⊕
Kathryn	⊕⊕⊕⊕⊕ ⊕⊕⊕
Mei	⊕⊕⊕⊕⊕ ⊕⊕⊕⊕⊕
Paul	⊕⊕⊕⊕⊕ ⊕⊕⊕⊕⊕
Raji	⊕⊕⊕⊕⊕ ⊕⊕⊕⊕⊕ ⊕⊕⊕⊕⊕
Sheeva	⊕⊕⊕⊕⊕ ⊕⊕⊕⊕⊕ ⊕⊕⊕⊕⊕ ⊕⊕⊕⊕⊕
Sheldon	⊕⊕⊕⊕⊕
Zimrat	⊕⊕⊕

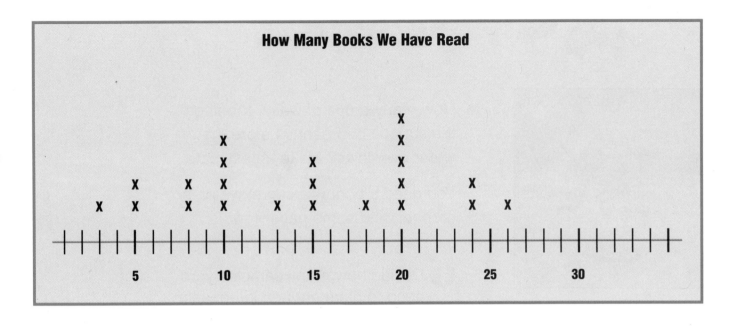

How Many Books We Have Read

2 • What can you find out from the sticker graph?

• What can you tell from the line plot?

• How would you choose to show the data?

• Do you think it is fair to give a sticker for each book read? Explain your thinking.

My Journal: Which display do you like better? Why? What questions do you have about displaying data?

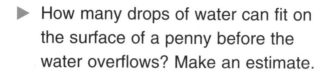

Analyzing Data

▶ How many drops of water can fit on the surface of a penny before the water overflows? Make an estimate.

You need a penny, a cup of water, a dropper, and some paper towels.

1 Decide how many samples you need to have enough information to make conclusions.

2 Record your data for each sample.

3 Make a line plot of the data collected by your group.

4 Write about what you observe in the data and any conclusions you can make.

ON YOUR OWN

In this First Nations game, Three Throw Ball, a person has three turns to throw a ball. First a ball is thrown just with the right arm, then with the left, and finally with both arms.

The trick: the thrower has to lie on her or his back to throw the ball.

Three Throw Ball
Distance Thrown (in metres)

Thrower	Right Arm	Left Arm	Both Arms
Anita	3.6	2.9	2.6
Graciela	4.3	3.6	3.0
Richard	2.9	4.7	3.2
Natasha	3.7	3.7	3.5
Cheryl	2.6	2.4	3.2
Seija	4.7	4.5	4.1
Eli	3.2	3.9	3.5
Josh	5.1	3.8	3.5
Claudette	3.3	3.3	3.3

1. How many people are playing Three Throw Ball?

2. Write as many statements as you can that describe the results of the Three Throw Ball game. Use the ideas you learned in this activity.

3. Is there anything surprising about the distances for throws using both arms?

4. *My Journal:* How do you think analyzing data helps you to discover things that were not obvious at first?

Practise Your Skills

Number Spun on Spinner

1. How many times was the spinner spun?
2. Which numbered sections on the spinner are probably about the same size?
3. If the experiment were repeated, would the new line plot look like this one? Explain.

Estimating Time

Fifteen students were asked how many minutes it takes them to get to school. The results of the survey are shown here.

22, 25, 12, 5, 15, 26, 38, 25,

20, 10, 30, 35, 18, 9, 20

These data can be arranged in a stem-and-leaf plot.

Stem	Leaves
0	5 9
1	0 2 5 8
2	0 0 2 5 5 6
3	0 5 8

▶ Why do you think this is called a stem-and-leaf plot?

Try this experiment. How long is one minute?

1 Close your eyes.

2 Your partner records the start time and says "go."

3 You say "stop" when you think exactly one minute has passed.

4 Your partner records the actual number of seconds that passed from the "go" to the "stop."

5 Repeat steps 1–4. Record the results separately from the first try.

6 Use the data from the whole class. Make two stem-and-leaf plots, one for each try.

7 Then make a bar graph for the first try. What information do you get from the stem-and-leaf plot that you do not get from the bar graph?

ON YOUR OWN

1. Look at the prices for CDs for 1994 and 1995.

Cost of the Top 25 CDs in 1995

$12.25	$13.50	$18.35
$11.49	$16.75	$12.75
$15.50	$11.69	$10.25
$15.25	$14.50	$17.99
$11.79	$13.35	$11.35
$14.25	$11.79	$12.99
$10.49	$16.50	$11.49
$12.75	$14.75	$11.99
	$10.99	

Cost of the Top 25 CDs in 1994

$12.55	$18.25	$14.25
$15.39	$17.35	$17.29
$13.49	$13.69	$14.25
$15.50	$13.69	$14.25
$16.99	$14.25	$13.99
$16.65	$12.69	$12.89
$13.99	$15.38	$17.69
$13.45	$15.75	$12.69
	$13.69	

1994 CD Prices

Stem	Leaves		
$18	.25		
$17	.29	.35	.69
$16	.65	.99	
$15			
$14			
$13			
$12			

1995 CD Prices

Stem	Leaves
$18	
$17	
$16	
$15	
$14	
$13	
$12	
$11	
$10	

a. Copy and complete these stem-and-leaf plots. Use the prices above.

b. Use your stem-and-leaf plots to write all the comparison statements you can. Explain any differences you see.

2. Look at the results for each race.

35	42	51	39	44	75	71	62	46	35
64	53	33	49	69	73	55	37	44	78

**The Sharks' Foot Race
(Time in seconds)**

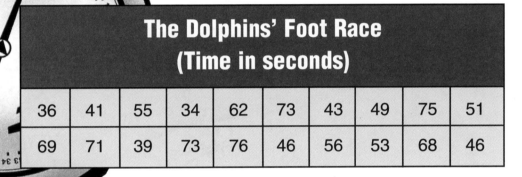

**The Dolphins' Foot Race
(Time in seconds)**

36	41	55	34	62	73	43	49	75	51
69	71	39	73	76	46	56	53	68	46

a. Make a stem-and-leaf plot for each table.

b. Write as many comparisons as you can about the foot races.

3. *My Journal:* Why might a stem-and-leaf plot be better than a bar graph for comparing data?

Practise Your Skills

The parents of the grade 5 students at Maple School are the following ages: 31, 36, 29, 30, 43, 38, 37, 40, 41, 52, 30, 35, 36, 37, 41, 40, 54, 30, 45, 34, 36, 50, 34, 39, 33, 42.

1. Make a stem-and-leaf plot to show the data.

2. Explain what the plot shows about the data.

Showing Temperature

Some cities in North America and their average temperatures

Whitehorse -1°c

YellowKnife -5°c

Iqaluit - 8°c

Calgary 4°c

Saskatoon 2°c

Brandon 2°c

Corner Brook 5°c

Vancouver 10°c

Windsor 9°c

Toronto 9°c

Quebec City 4°c

Sherbrooke 4°c

Saint John 7°c

Halifax

Chicago 9°c

San Francisco 14°c

Denver 10°c

Detroit 9°c

13°c New York City

Dallas·Ft·Worth 19°c

16°c Atlanta

24°c Miami

Honolulu 25°c

Mexico·City 16°c

27°c Acapulco

City	Mean June High Temperature (°C)	Mean June Low Temperature (°C)
Brandon, MB	23	9
Calgary, AB	20	7
Charlottetown, PE	18	9
Corner Brook, NF	18	8
Grand Falls, NB	21	10
Halifax, NS: Citadel	19	10
Halifax, NS: Airport	20	9
Honolulu, HI	31	18
Iqaluit, Nunavut	8	2
Miami, FL	32	22
Phoenix, AZ	41	4
Quebec City, QC	22	10
San Juan, PR	29	21
Saskatoon, SK	23	9
Sherbrooke, QC	22	8
Toronto, ON: City	24	14
Toronto, ON: Airport	24	11
Vancouver, BC	19	11
White Horse, YT	18	5
Windsor, ON	25	14
Yellowknife, NT	18	8

ON YOUR OWN

Volcano Name	Metres Above Sea Level	Last Major Eruption
Cinder Cone	2107	1851
Lassen Peak	3188	1921
Mt. Shasta	4319	1855
Mt. Hood	3430	1801
Mt. Baker	3287	1870
Mt. Rainier	4395	1882
Mt. St. Helens	2551	1984
Haleakala	3058	1790
Hualalai	2517	1801
Kilauea	1248	1984
Mauna Loa	4712	1984
Kiska	1228	1969
Little Sitkin	1203	1828
Cerberus	781	1873
Gareloi	1638	1930
Tanaga	1807	1914
Kanaga	1357	1933
Great Sitkin	1761	1945
Keniuji	270	1828

1. The data on the right are displayed in a table. Choose another way to display the data. Then write five questions about your display. Exchange your display and questions with a classmate. Answer each other's questions.

2. **My Journal:** Explain why you think stem-and-leaf plots are useful.

Comparing Data

▶ The charts on pages 161 to 163 show the approximate lengths of 65 different dinosaurs. Use this information to make a stem-and-leaf plot.
Then make a line plot.

Compsognathus	1 m
Ornitholestes	2 m
Coelophysis	3 m
Oviraptor	2 m
Struthiomimus	4 m
Dromiceiomimus	4 m
Segisaurus	1 m
Avimimus	2 m
Segnosaur	5 m
Stenonychosaurus	2 m
Saurornithoides	2 m
Ceratosaurus	6 m
Dilophosaurus	6 m

Allosaurus	12 m
Tyrannosaurus	14 m
Daspletosaurus	9 m
Albertosaurus	9 m
Anchisaurus	3 m
Plateosaurus	7 m
Apatosaurus	21 m
Diplodocus	27 m
Camarasaurus	18 m
Brachiosaurus	23 m
Opisthocoelicaudia	12 m
Saltasaurus	12 m
Vulcanodon	6 m

Lesothosaurus	1 m
Heterodontosaurus	2 m
Scutellosaurus	2 m
Hypsilophodon	2 m
Dryosaurus	4 m
Tenontosaurus	6 m
Camptosaurus	6 m
Ouranosaurus	7 m
Muttaburrasaurus	7 m
Iguanodon	10 m
Bactrosaurus	5 m
Kritosaurus	9 m
Anatosaurus	10 m

Edmontosaurus	10 m
Protoceratops	2 m
Psittacosaurus	2 m
Tsintaosaurus	7 m
Saurolophus	11 m
Corythosaurus	10 m
Parasaurolophus	10 m
Styracosaurus	6 m
Centrosaurus	6 m
Triceratops	9 m
Chasmosaurus	5 m
Anchiceratops	6 m
Pentaceratops	7 m

Torosaurus	7 m
Stegoceras	2 m
Homalocephale	3 m
Pachycephalosaurus	8 m
Stegosaurus	7 m
Tuojiangosaurus	6 m
Kentrosaurus	3 m
Scelidosaurus	4 m
Hylaeosaurus	4 m
Polacanthus	4 m
Nodosaurus	6 m
Pinacosaurus	5 m
Euoplocephalus	6 m

Understanding Means and Medians

The mean and median masses for different types of deer are given on these pages.

Lapland Reindeer

1 m tall
mean: 136 kg
median: 139 kg

Alaskan Moose

2 m high at the shoulder
mean: 750 kg
median: 739 kg

Japanese Sika

0.76 m tall
mean: 36 kg
median: 34 kg

American Elk

1.5 m high at the shoulder
mean: 386 kg
median: 398 kg

Caribou

1 m tall
mean: 136 kg
median: 136 kg

Indian Barasingha

1.5 m high at the shoulder
mean: 205 kg
median: 200 kg

Indian Sambar

over 1.5 m tall
mean: 318 kg
median: 330 kg

Chilean Rabbit Deer

0.3 m tall
mean: 9 kg
median: 10 kg

165

ON YOUR OWN

1. Create a set of six numbers for which the median is greater than the mean.

2. Tell whether each statement is true or false.

   a. The mean is always one of the numbers in a list of numbers.

   b. Mean and average are the same.

   c. The mean and the median are always the same.

   d. If there is one middle number in a list, it is the median.

   e. The mode only appears once in a list of numbers.

3. Find the mean height of the people in your household.

4. Use mental math to estimate the mean for these numbers: 95, 187, 220, 230, 299, 302, 489, 575.

5. *My Journal:* What questions do you still have about the mean, median, and mode?

information From
Cords to CARDS

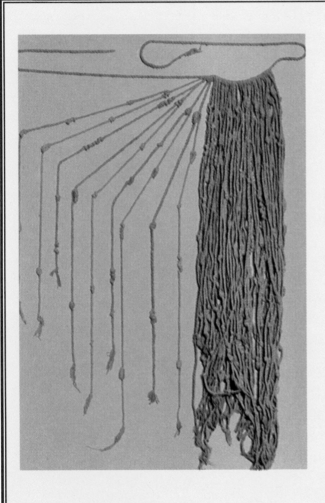

Have you ever wondered how people analyzed census data before they had computers?

Years ago, the Inca in Peru used knotted ropes called quipu. The quipu used a decimal system. A knot in a row farthest from the main rope indicated 1. The next knot closer in represented 10, and so on. To show the population on a quipu, different colours were used for men, women, and children.

In the 1911 census in Canada, information was collected on punch cards. They were used on a pantograph, a kind of data processing machine. By 1961, the computer was used for Canada's census.

1. What do you think the benefits were of using punch cards?

2. Why do you think computers are now used to store data for the census? What are the advantages?

3. Invent your own method of recording and storing data on a cord or a card.

Representing Change with a Graph

Materials:

Cardboard tube from
a roll of paper towels
Metre stick
Tape

1 Tape the metre stick to the wall. Place the zero line about 1 m from the floor.

2 Measure 3 m from the wall. Use tape to mark this spot on the floor.

3 Stand with the toes of your shoes on the tape on the floor.

4 Look through the tube. Record the length of the metre stick you see. You will need to subtract the lesser number from the greater number.

5 Repeat this experiment several times. Move the tape on the floor to 2.5 m, 2.0 m, and so on, from the wall. Record the distances on the floor and the lengths you see. Draw a graph to represent these data.

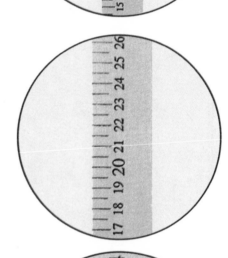

Use the data below. Different tubes were used to generate the data. Follow the directions. Answer the questions to find which tube was used for each set of data.

Distance from wall (in metres)	SET 1 Length observed (cm)	SET 2 Length observed (cm)	SET 3 Length observed (cm)
0.5	15	10	6
1.0	28	19	12
1.5	45	29	19
2.0	62	41	25
2.5	78	53	31
3.0	94	63	37

1. Construct a broken-line graph for each set of data.

2. Suppose the tube that generated the Set 1 data were placed 1.75 m from the wall. What length of the metre stick might you see? Explain.

3. Use the tube that generated the Set 2 data. How far do you think you would have to be from the wall to see the entire metre stick? Explain.

4. Use the tube that generated the Set 3 data. About how much of the metre stick would you see at a distance of 4 m?

5. Match Tubes A, B, and C to Set 1, Set 2, and Set 3. Explain your reasoning.

6. *My Journal:* What can you learn from the graphs the class made?

TUBES

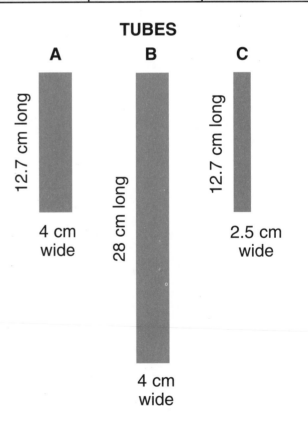

A
12.7 cm long
4 cm wide

B
28 cm long
4 cm wide

C
12.7 cm long
2.5 cm wide

The Time in a Week

How do you spend the time in a week? Estimate the times for different activities. Then keep track to check your estimates.

Choose one activity. Then write a questionnaire to collect data. Display the survey results in a graph. Analyze the results.

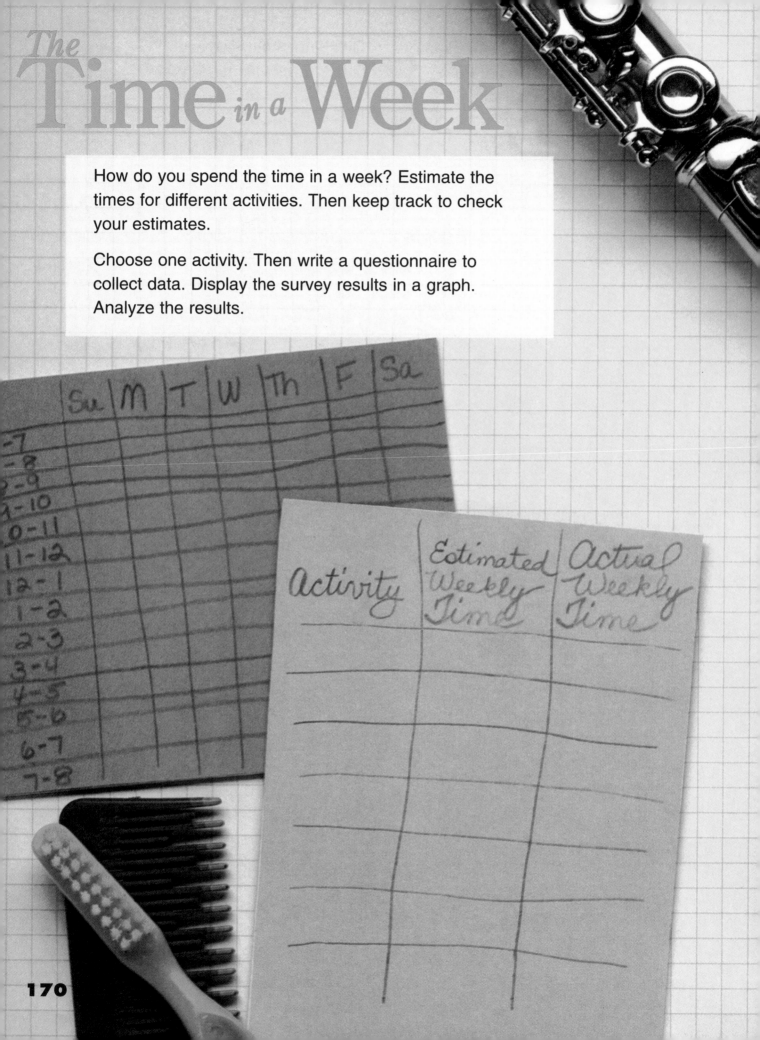

	Su	M	T	W	Th	F	Sa
-7							
-8							
-9							
-10							
0-11							
11-12							
12-1							
1-2							
2-3							
3-4							
4-5							
5-6							
6-7							
7-8							

Activity	Estimated Weekly Time	Actual Weekly Time

CheckYOURSELF

Great job! You collected the data thoroughly and accurately. The graph you chose to display your data gave a good picture. You wrote to explain the data and how you analyzed the data.

PROBLEM BANK

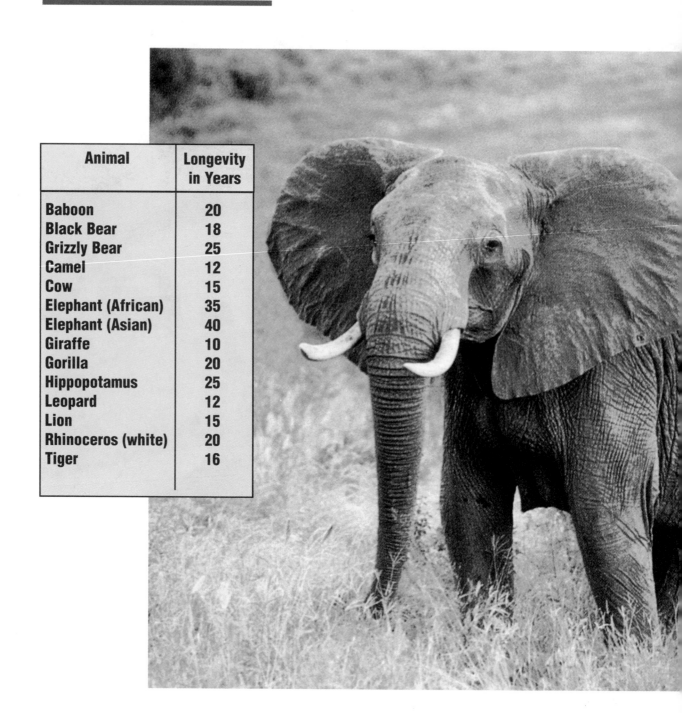

Animal	Longevity in Years
Baboon	20
Black Bear	18
Grizzly Bear	25
Camel	12
Cow	15
Elephant (African)	35
Elephant (Asian)	40
Giraffe	10
Gorilla	20
Hippopotamus	25
Leopard	12
Lion	15
Rhinoceros (white)	20
Tiger	16

1. The longevity of an African elephant is 35 years. This means that the typical African elephant lives about 35 years. The table shows the longevities of some familiar animals.

   a. Construct a stem-and-leaf plot showing the longevities of these animals.

   b. Use your stem-and-leaf plot to find the mean and median longevities.

2. One Asian elephant died at 70 years of age. Does this prove that the longevity for Asian elephants given in the table is incorrect? Explain your thinking.

3. Find out which animal has the greatest longevity. Is the longevity of this animal greater than the longevity of humans?

PROBLEM BANK

Northeast Division	
Team	Points
Pittsburgh	101
Boston	97
Montreal	96
Buffalo	95
Quebec	76
Hartford	63
Ottawa	37

Central Division	
Team	Points
Detroit	100
Toronto	98
Dallas	97
St. Louis	91
Chicago	87
Winnipeg	57

Atlantic Division	
Team	Points
NY Rangers	112
New Jersey	106
Washington	88
NY Islanders	84
Florida	83
Philadelphia	80
Tampa Bay	71

Pacific Division	
Team	Points
Calgary	97
Vancouver	85
San Jose	82
Anaheim	71
Los Angeles	66
Edmonton	64

These tables show the final standing of the teams in the
National Hockey League in 1994. A team gets 2 points for
a win and 1 point for a tie. There are no points for a loss.
The team with the greatest number of points wins.

4. Which team in the NHL finished the season with the most points? They tied 8 games. How many games did they win?

5. Vancouver won 41 games. How many games did they tie?

6. For each division, make a stem-and-leaf plot to show how many points were scored by the teams in that division.

7. Use your stem-and-leaf plots from exercise 6. Find the median number of points in each division. (Remember that the median of 6 numbers is the mean of the two middle numbers when the numbers are arranged in order.)

8. Which division of the NHL had the greatest median number of points? For which division was the mean number of points greatest?

9. Make a stem-and-leaf plot. Show the points of all 26 teams in the NHL. What was the median number of points earned?

10. Compare the median number of points earned by teams east of Chicago with the median number earned by teams west of and including Chicago.

11. The mode is the number of points that were earned by the most teams. Make a line plot of the points earned by the 26 teams. Record the mode.

12. To which division of the NHL do you think the year's Stanley Cup winner belonged? Give reasons for your answer.

S K I L L
BANK
FROM THIS UNIT

1. Here are the average heights of broadleaf trees native
   to Canada: 15 m, 27 m, 6 m, 21 m, 12 m, 21 m, 21 m, 18 m,
   12 m, 15 m, 6 m, 27 m, 9 m, 27 m, 12 m, 21 m, 21 m, 21 m,
   12 m, 18 m, 21 m, 6 m, 9 m, 6 m, 30 m, 33 m, 21 m, 9 m, 15 m.
   a. What is the range of the data?
   b. Examine the measures listed. How might you number
       a line plot?
   c. Make a line plot to show the data.

2. The students in a grade 5 class received these marks on
   a test: 74, 75, 78, 82, 80, 88, 68, 90, 65, 75, 70, 62, 91,
   76, 74, 83, 95, 60, 79, 82.
   a. In a stem-and-leaf plot, what would you use for the
       stem?
   b. Make a stem-and-leaf plot to show the data.

3. Marty earned $3.50 one week, $2.25 the next week,
   $3.25 the third week, $2.00 the fourth week, and
   $3.00 the fifth week.
   a. What were his mean weekly earnings?
   b. What was the median amount he earned?

4. **a.** When graphing the data
       on the right, how might you
       number the axis that shows
       the mass?
   b. Make a broken-line graph
       to show the data.

Age	Average Mass (kilograms)
2	12
4	16
6	19
8	24
10	32
12	41

SKILL BANK
LOOKING BACK

1. Name the fraction shaded.

a.   **b.** 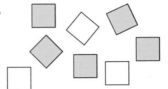   **c.**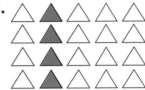

2. Name the mixed number.

a.   **b.** 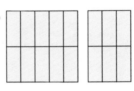   **c.**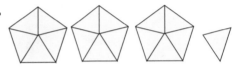

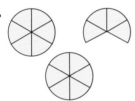

3. Copy and complete the equivalent fractions.

a. $\frac{3}{4} = \frac{\blacksquare}{8}$ **b.** $\frac{2}{3} = \frac{\blacksquare}{12}$ **c.** $\frac{1}{4} = \frac{\blacksquare}{24}$ **d.** $\frac{3}{5} = \frac{\blacksquare}{20}$

e. $\frac{7}{10} = \frac{\blacksquare}{50}$ **f.** $\frac{5}{6} = \frac{\blacksquare}{18}$ **g.** $\frac{1}{8} = \frac{\blacksquare}{32}$ **h.** $\frac{5}{8} = \frac{\blacksquare}{16}$

4. Copy each expression. Write < or > in place of each ■.

a. 3.8 ■ 8.3   **b.** 91.3 ■ 9.3   **c.** 40.6 ■ 39.4

d. 51.5 ■ 55.1   **e.** 68.2 ■ 82.6   **f.** 52 ■ 9.5

5. Calculate.

a. 2.67 + 3.8   **b.** 65.4 − 47.3   **c.** 91.2 − 24.6

d. 38.5 + 4.7   **e.** 56 − 1.4   **f.** 73.2 − 5.1

g. 8.8 + 12.6 + 0.45   **h.** 34 + 16.9 + 5.82

6. Estimate. Then calculate.

a. 9.3 × 5   **b.** 4.75 × 6   **c.** 3 × 19.2   **d.** 7 × 4.9

e. 47.2 × 9   **f.** 2 × 98.51   **g.** 74.1 × 4   **h.** 83.5 × 8

i. 6.5 ÷ 5   **j.** 78.6 ÷ 3   **k.** 5.2 ÷ 4   **l.** 92.16 ÷ 8

m. 2.2 ÷ 4   **n.** 10.8 ÷ 9   **o.** 23.17 ÷ 7   **p.** 32.4 ÷ 6

Spinner 1

red
~~IIII~~ III

blu~~e~~
III

Spinner 2

circles
~~IIII~~ ~~IIII~~ III

stars
~~IIII~~ ~~IIII~~ III
~~IIII~~ IIII

*H*ow likely is it?

MAKING PREDICTIONS

S·T·A·R·T·I·N·G OUT

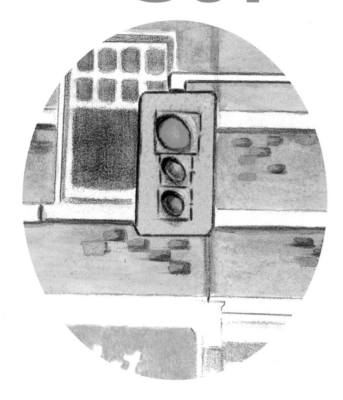

1 • Tell what you see in each picture. What other possibilities are there for the event in each picture?

• What other picture could you add to this page that shows one of many possibilities?

• What other situation can you think of in which two possibilities are equally likely?

My Journal: When might you want to know how likely an event is?

Describing the Likelihood of Events

▶ How likely is each event?

In some cases, you may need to collect some data to have a better idea of how likely the event is.

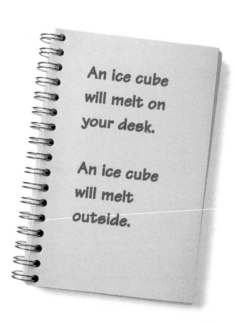

An ice cube will melt on your desk.

An ice cube will melt outside.

It will rain this week.

It will snow this week.

The sun will set before 7 o'clock.

The sun will rise before 7 o'clock.

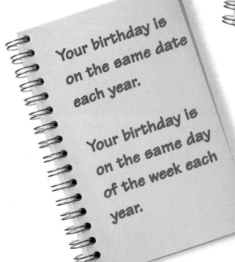

Your birthday is on the same date each year.

Your birthday is on the same day of the week each year.

Someone in the class is over 50 years old.

Someone in the class is younger than 50 years old.

Spinner Experiments

▶ How would you describe each spinner?

▶ What do you think would be the result of
50 spins on each spinner?

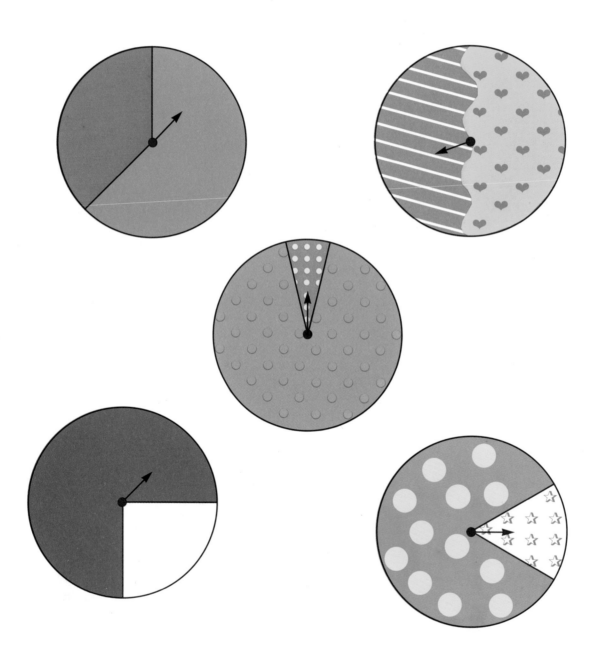

▶ Here are some spinners that a group of students think will give them the results they want.

- Choose one of the spinners and make one just like it.
- Decide on the number of times you should spin the spinner. Then spin to find which outcome is most likely.
- What does your data tell you? Will the students be disappointed?

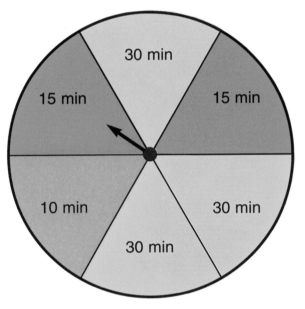

Spin for the length of today's recess.
(We want a long one!)

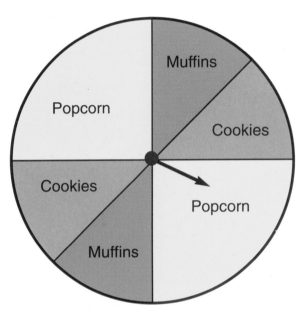

Spin to decide on tomorrow's treat.
(We love popcorn!)

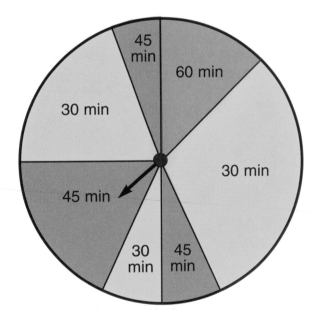

Spin for the amount of tonight's homework.
(We want less homework!)

1. Use the terms below. Describe the likelihood of spinning each colour on this spinner.

   equally likely
   more likely
   less likely
   always
   never

   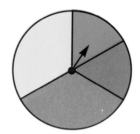

2. Design a spinner that has four outcomes that are equally likely. Then design another one that looks different from the first, but still has four equally likely outcomes.

3. Imagine that you can spin a spinner each week to determine what chores you have to do at home. Design a spinner that you think your parents would like, but that you predict will give you chores you don't mind doing.

4. *My Journal:* What have you learned about probability from experimenting with spinners?

Practise Your Skills

Match a spinner to each expression.

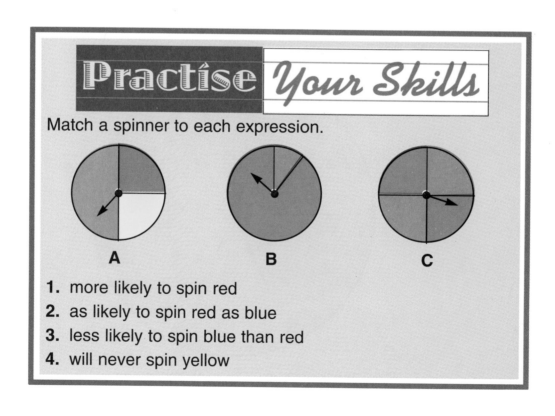

A   B   C

1. more likely to spin red
2. as likely to spin red as blue
3. less likely to spin blue than red
4. will never spin yellow

Making Predictions

```
        5 3 # # $ 3 0 5
      ) ) 6 * ; 4 8 2 6 ) 4 #
    . ) 4 # ; 8 0 6 * ; 4 8 $ 8
    @ 6 0 ) ) 8 5 ; & # ( ; : # *
  8 $ 8 3 ( 8 8 ) 5 * $ ; 4 6 ( ; 8
  8 * 9 6 * ? ; 8 ) * # ( ; 4 8 5 )
; 5 * $ 2 : * # ( ; 4 9 5 6 * 2 ( 5 *
 − 4 ) 8 @ 8 * ; 4 0 6 9 2 8 5 ) ; )
  6 $ 8 ) 4 # # ; & ( # 9 ; 4 8 0 8
  & ; 8 : 8 # & ; 4 8 $ 8 5 ; 4 ) 4
    8 5 $ 5 2 8 8 0 6 * 8 & ( # 9 ;
      4 8 ; ( 8 8 ; 4 ( # ? 3 4 ;
      4 8 ) 4 # ; & 6 & ; : & 8
            8 ; # ? ;
```

10 000 words. How many would be in a story using 50 000 words? Would you want to check your predictions?

Now think about other languages. What do you think would be the most common letters in French? Are there languages whose letters or symbols you don't know? If you or any of your classmates know a language other than English, discuss how to find the most-used letters or symbols.

Have you ever wondered which five letters are used most often in the English language?

Make a guess. Write down the letters.

How could you check your guess? What size sample should you check? How should you begin? If you work with a group, you can share the work. After you have completed your sample, predict how many of each letter you would find in an article using

1 Why would code makers and code breakers be interested in what letters appear most often?

2 The code above was used by Edgar Allan Poe in "The Gold Bug." Can you use what you learned about letters in English to break it?

3 People in one part of London, England, are called Cockneys. They use 3 different codes to communicate – Rhyming Slang, Back Slang, and Centre Slang. Find out more about one of these codes.

THE RANDOM Removal GAME

Group

Pairs or a small group

Materials

- 15 counters per player
- 2 number cubes, each labelled 1 to 6

Goal

To remove all your counters first

Rules

1 Each player makes a number line from 2 to 12.

2 Each player makes a line plot by placing 15 counters above numbers on the line, according to the likelihood of that sum being rolled.

If you roll two number cubes labelled 1 to 6, the possible sums are 2 to 12.

3 To play, a player rolls the two number cubes and states the sum. He or she removes one counter from that position on her or his number line. If there are no counters at that position, no counter is removed on that turn.

4 Players take turns rolling the cubes, until a player has removed all of her or his counters.

ON YOUR OWN

1. Write a note to someone who is about to play Random Removal for the first time. Tell the person how you think the counters should be placed. Tell why and try to be convincing!

2. Make a list of games you like to play. Think of how you play them. Write to explain the part skill plays in these games and the part chance plays.

3. Suppose you roll two number cubes labelled 1 to 6. How likely is it that you will get a sum that is:
   a. less than 3?
   b. greater than 7?
   c. 7?

4. *My Journal:* What questions do you have about finding possible outcomes?

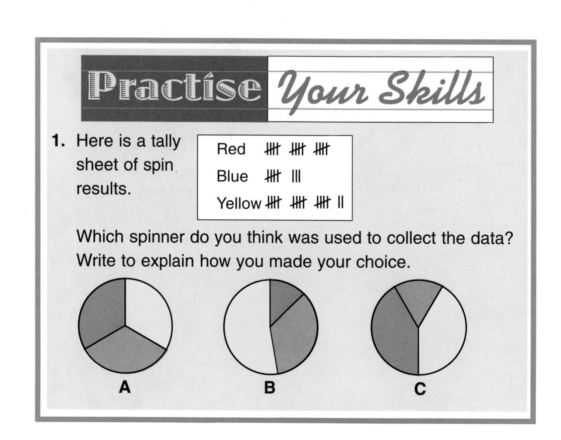

Practise Your Skills

1. Here is a tally sheet of spin results.

Red													
Blue								
Yellow															

Which spinner do you think was used to collect the data? Write to explain how you made your choice.

A   B   C

Probability Experiments

▶ What are the possible outcomes?

▶ Which are more likely?
less likely? equally likely?

Here are some experiments. Find the possible outcomes. Then collect data to find how likely each outcome is.

1. Dropping a Folded Paper

Cut out a square. Fold it as shown below. How could it land? How does it land? Describe the outcomes.

2. Dropping a Paper Cup

Choose a height. Drop
a paper cup. What possible
ways can it land?
How does it land?

3. Dropping a Tack

How can a tack land?
Is one way more likely?

4. *My Journal:* How do you use the data you collect to make statements about the likelihood of the outcomes?

Skill and Chance

Think about the games you have played. Some involve skill, while others involve chance. Still others involve a combination of skill and chance.

equally likely

likely

RULES

always

1.

Materials
• paper
•

never

Now it is your turn to invent a game.
The game must use numbers on
cubes or other solids. It can involve
addition, subtraction, multiplication,
or division.

Explain your game as clearly
as you can. Be sure to tell about:

- materials
- group size
- how you decide who starts
- how you play
- how to keep score.

CheckYOURSELF

Great job! You invented a game that is fun to play.
Your descriptions of the materials, group size, and rules
are clear. Your report explains the role of chance and
skill in your game. It makes sense and is complete.

MAKING PREDICTIONS

1. Describe a situation in which there are only a few possible outcomes. Tell whether you think each outcome is more likely, less likely, or equally likely.

2. Is it possible to flip a coin 20 times and have it land heads every time? Is it impossible? What do you think is likely?

3. The choices for a class sports day are soccer, baseball, or relay games. Design a six-part spinner that you think will result in your choice of sport winning more often than not.

4. Here are two Snack Spinners. Which would you spin to decide on your snack? Explain.

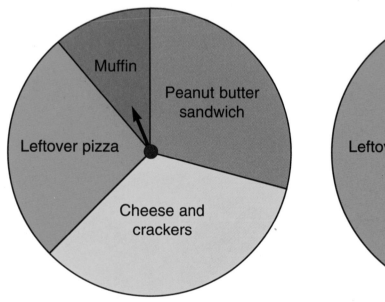

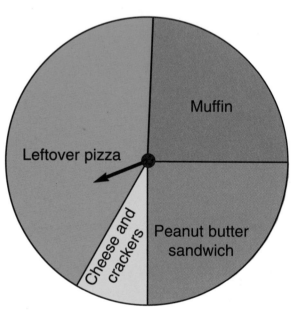

5. Copy the chart. For each event, write other possible outcomes.

Event	Possible Outcomes
A hockey game is played between the Blues and the Reds.	• The Blues win. • •
Two coins are tossed.	• One lands heads; the other lands tails. • •
There is a knock at the classroom door.	• It is the school principal. • •

6. Imagine you are playing a game that involves rolling two number cubes labelled 1 to 6. Describe how likely it is that you will roll a double.

7. A game called Pig involves rolling number cubes and adding the results. You play in pairs. The goal is to try to be the first to reach a total of 100. On your turn, you roll the number cubes as many times as you like, keeping a running total of the sum. When you stop, you record the total for your turn. Add this total to the totals from previous turns. However, if you roll a 1 before you stop, your score for that roll is 0. If you roll two 1s, your turn ends, and your total score for the game so far goes back to 0. Play the game. What game strategy would you use? Write to explain it.

S K I L L
BANK
FROM THIS UNIT

1. Match the tallies to the spinners. Explain your choices.

A	B	C
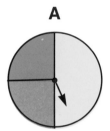		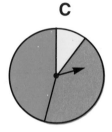

1

Red	Blue	Yellow
⪫⪫	⪫⪫	⪫⪫
⪫⪫	⪫⪫	
IIII	I	

2

Red	Blue	Yellow
⪫⪫	⪫⪫	⪫⪫
⪫⪫	⪫⪫	IIII
I		

3

Red	Blue	Yellow
⪫⪫	⪫⪫	⪫⪫
II	IIII	⪫⪫
		IIII

2. Use each of these words in a sentence.
possible
always
never
probable

3. Use these terms to describe
the outcomes on each spinner.
equally likely
more likely
less likely

A   B

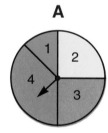 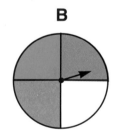

4. Which do you think is more likely? Explain your answer.
- The next person to walk into the classroom
will be an adult.
- The next person to walk into the classroom
will be a student.

1. Write each as a decimal number.

    a. sixteen hundredths   **b.** four hundredths

    c. eight and three tenths   **d.** twenty and two hundredths

2. Order the numbers from least to greatest.

    a. 21.1, 12.1, 21.2, 1.22, 22.1   **b.** 9.8, 8.9, 89, 0.98, 1.09

3. Estimate. Then calculate.

    a. $4.11 + 0.7$ **b.** $32 + 0.9$ **c.** $56.2 + 3.8$ **d.** $27.4 + 58.6$

    e. $0.97 - 0.62$ **f.** $8.5 - 4$ **g.** $19.2 - 10.1$ **h.** $73.4 - 51.8$

    i. 8.4×7 **j.** 15.2×2 **k.** 31.72×6 **l.** 86.3×5

    m. $10.2 \div 3$ **n.** $18.0 \div 5$ **o.** $33.6 \div 6$ **p.** $44.17 \div 7$

4. In the first seven softball games Janette played this season, she had 3, 2, 4, 2, 2, 1, and 3 hits.

    a. What number of hits is the mode?

    b. What number of hits is the median?

5. One day the temperature went from 8°C at 6:00 a.m., to 10°C at 10:00 a.m., to 15°C at 2:00 p.m., to 9°C at 6:00 p.m. Make a broken-line graph to show the data.

6. Here is a record of the number of books students in one class read over the summer.

    Li, 6   Joanne, 7   Alice, 3   Ria, 9   Sue, 6   Coreen, 6

    May, 14   Pat, 5   Bill, 2   Arn, 10   Tom, 4   Peg, 3

    Roy, 2   Max, 5   Janet, 7   Rob, 1   Ana, 5   Pamela, 6

    Make a line plot to show the data.

What can measurements tell us?

1 • What measurements would you make to describe the size of this garden?

• The stakes are 1 m apart. Tell how long and wide you think the entire garden is.

• Do you think there is enough fencing to enclose the entire garden? Explain your thinking.

• Do you think there is enough fertilizer for the entire garden? Explain your thinking.

• Compare the size of this garden with your classroom. How do they compare?

My Journal: When did you need to know a measurement for an object? How did you measure?

16m

FERTILIZER COVERS 5m²

203

Measuring Many Dimensions

It's time for a
SCAVENGER HUNT!

Here is your list.
Find an object for each
of these measures.

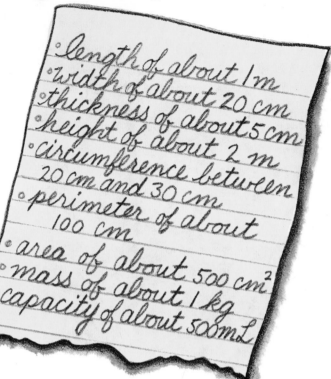

- length of about 1 m
- width of about 20 cm
- thickness of about 5 cm
- height of about 2 m
- circumference between 20 cm and 30 cm
- perimeter of about 100 cm
- area of about 500 cm²
- mass of about 1 kg
- capacity of about 500 mL

▶ Use a chart like this to record your findings.

Looking For	Item Found	Actual Measurement
height of about 2 m		
length of about 1 m		
width of about 20 cm		

Words to Know

Area: the number of square units needed to cover a figure

*Each square unit is one square centimetre.
So the area is 12 cm².*

Perimeter: the distance around a figure

*2 cm + 6 cm + 2 cm + 6 cm = 16 cm
The perimeter of this rectangle is 16 cm.*

6 cm

2 cm   2 cm

6 cm

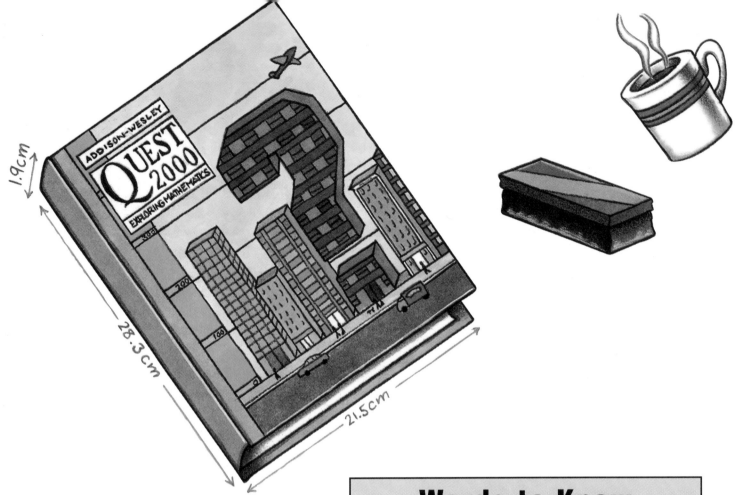

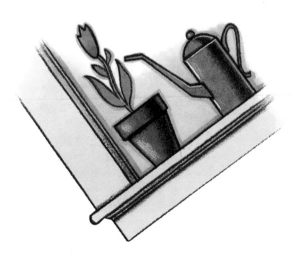

Words to Know

Circumference: the distance around a circle

circumference, about 50 mm

50 mm

Mass: the amount of matter in an object

Some units of mass are grams (g), kilograms (kg), and tonnes (t).
1000 g = 1 kg
1000 kg = 1 t

Capacity: the amount a container can hold

Some units of capacity are millilitres (mL) and litres (L).
1000 mL = 1 L

1. Interview people. Find out the kinds of things they measure at work, at home, or while playing sports or doing hobbies. Make a chart to record your findings.

Thing Measured	Why Measured	Tool Used	Unit Used

2. Choose an object. Measure as many of its attributes as you can. Draw it and include all your measures.

3. Find a can. Estimate whether the height is greater or less than the circumference. Measure to find out. Record what you find. Estimate and measure other cans. Describe any pattern you see.

4. Suppose you want a poster for your room.
What size could it be?

5.

a. What was measured to give the size on the can?
What was measured to give the size on the box?

b. About how many boxes of cereal are needed to fill an order for 5 kg?

c. A school needs 25 L of juice for snack time. How many cans this size should the school get?

6. *My Journal:* What questions do you have about measuring?

Practise Your Skills

1. Write the symbol for the unit you would use for each measure.

a. the length of a baseball bat

b. the mass of a newborn kitten

c. the thickness of a nickel

d. the distance between two cities

e. the capacity of a pail

f. the mass of a truck

g. the capacity of a thimble

h. the mass of a bag of potatoes

2. What tools would you use to measure these?

a. the length of a football field

b. the width of a postage stamp

c. the mass of a hamster

d. the mass of a dog

e. the capacity of a glass

f. the capacity of a bathtub

Exploring Perimeter and Area

▶ Here are some tile designs. What is the area and the perimeter of each design?

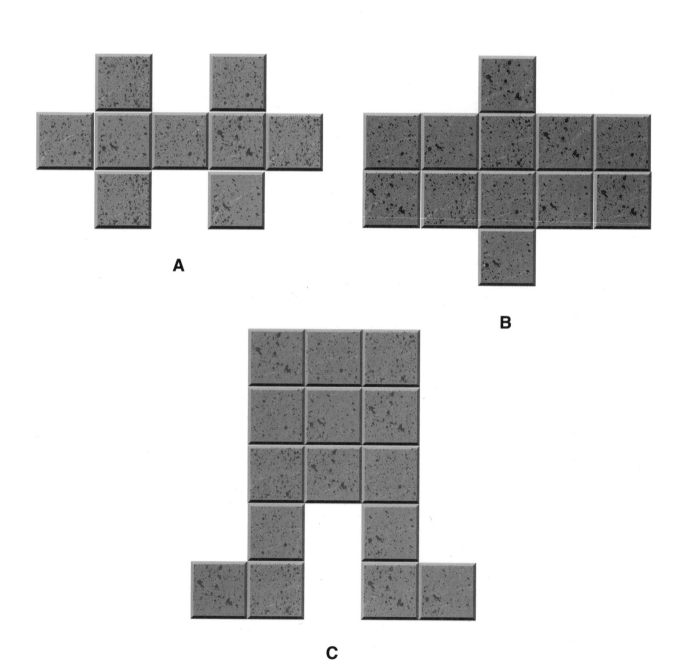

A

B

C

▶ Look at the three tile designs on page 206. Then try this:

- For each design, make a new design that has the same area but shorter perimeter.

- For each design, make a new design that has the same perimeter, but greater area.

- For each design, make a new design that has the same area and the same perimeter, but a different shape.

- Remove a tile from each design so that each perimeter is greater than it was.

ON YOUR OWN

Now it is your turn to make some different designs.

1. Use tiles. Make a design that has an area of 6 square units and a perimeter of 14 units.

2. Make a design with an area of 6 square units, and a perimeter of 12 units.

3. Make a design with an area of 6 square units, and a perimeter of 10 units.

4. Which of your designs would you recommend for the shape of a swimming pool? Explain your thinking.

5. *My Journal:* Do figures with the same area have the same perimeter? Explain.

Perimeters and Areas of Irregular Figures

Here are some techniques for finding the approximate area of an irregular figure.

1 Count the squares that are completely within the figure. Add each square that has more than one half within the figure. Don't count any square that has less than one half within the figure.

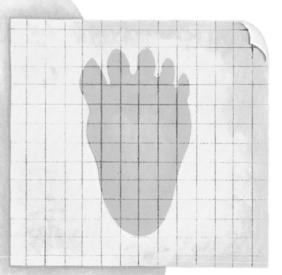

2 Draw as large a rectangle as you can within the figure. Draw other smaller rectangles that fit. Find the number of squares in the rectangles. For every two partial squares, add one square unit.

3 Enclose the figure with a rectangle. Count the squares in the rectangle. Subtract each square that has more than one half outside of the figure.

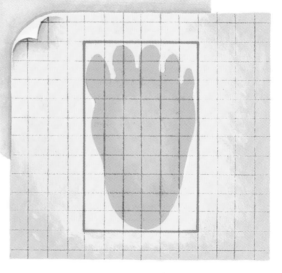

Here are some techniques for finding the approximate perimeter of an irregular figure.

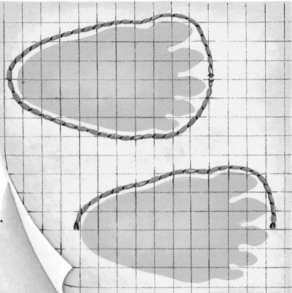

1 Lay string along the edge of the figure. Then measure the string.

2 Lay string around one half the figure. Double the string. Then measure it.

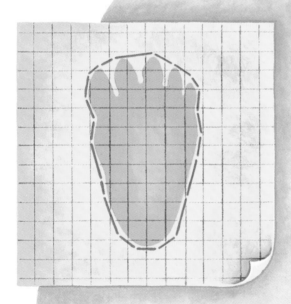

3 Outline the figure using straight line segments. Count the segments that are about 1 square long. Add 2 for each segment that is about 2 squares long. Add $\frac{1}{2}$ for each segment that is about one half as long as a square.

- What other methods can you suggest?
- Which methods do you think are the most accurate?
- Which method do you like best?

Here is a map of some islands in the Strait of Georgia.

Powell River

Strait of

Texada
Island

Denman
Island

Comox

Hornby
Island

Lasqueti
Island

Qualicum
Beach

Georg

SCALE
1 cm = 5 km

1. Which island on page 210 has the longest coastline? Explain your thinking.

2. What is the approximate area of Denman Island? Lasqueti Island?

3. On grid paper, draw an island whose area is less than the area of the largest island shown on page 210, but greater than the area of the smallest island. Explain how you know that your island's area is within that range.

4. Choose one island on page 210. Draw another island that has about the same perimeter but a different area.

5. *My Journal:* Explain your method of finding the area of an irregular figure.

Practíse Your Skills

1. Measure to find the perimeter. Give your answer in centimetres.

   a.

   b.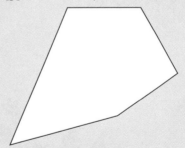

2. Find the approximate area. Give your answer in square units.

   a.

   b.

Same Area, Different Perimeters

Here are aerial views of some playgrounds.

▶ How would you describe them?

▶ Which do you think give children more room to play?

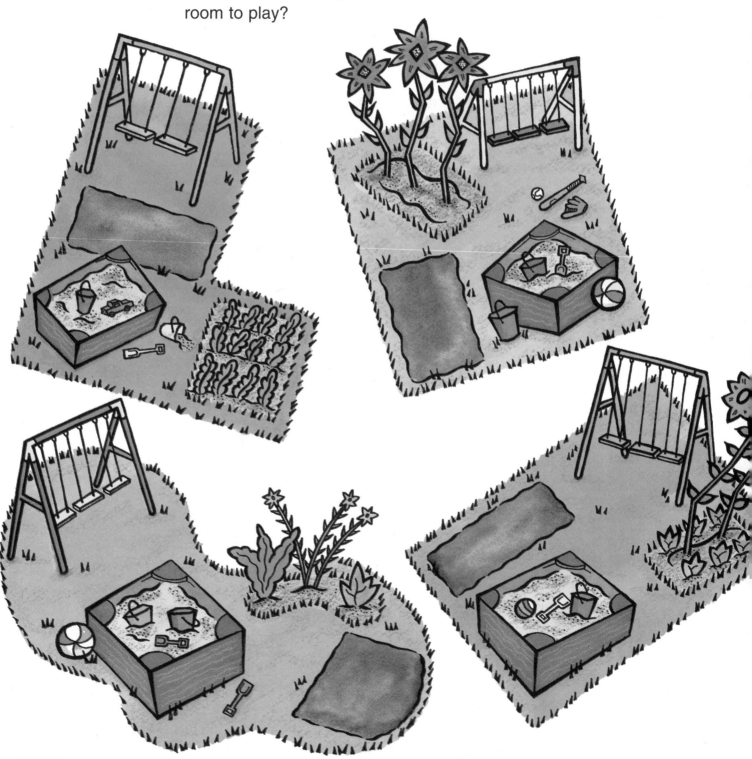

1. Use centimetre grid paper. Show all the rectangles that have an area of 24 cm². Which has the longest perimeter? Which has the shortest perimeter?

2. A developer is planning to provide a 30-m² garden with each house she builds. The garden is not attached to the house. It will be surrounded by decorative fencing. What garden shape would save on the cost of the fencing? Explain your thinking.

3. *My Journal:* What do you know about the perimeters of figures with the same area?

Practise Your Skills

1. Use 8 square tiles. Make figures with each perimeter.
   a. 12 units   **b.** 14 units   **c.** 16 units   **d.** 18 units

2. Find the area of each figure in the pair. Which has the greater perimeter?

   a.

   b.

Same Perimeter, Different Areas

▶ You have some boards that total 20 m in length.
You want to use them to enclose a rectangular sandbox.
What size can you make the sandbox?

1. Find an object that you think has a perimeter less than 50 cm. Measure the perimeter to the nearest centimetre. Draw two rectangles that have about the same perimeter as the object.

2. How many different rectangles with a perimeter of 16 cm can you find? Show them on grid paper.

3. Tobias needs exactly 28 m of edging to go around the outside of his garden plot. What could the area of his garden be? Give two answers.

4. What is the largest area you can enclose with a 36-m ball of string? What is the smallest area you can enclose with it? Explain your thinking.

5. *My Journal:* Do figures with the same perimeter have the same area? Explain.

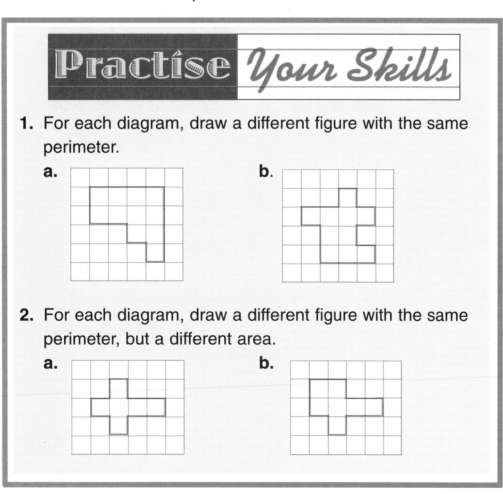

Practise Your Skills

1. For each diagram, draw a different figure with the same perimeter.

   a.   b.

2. For each diagram, draw a different figure with the same perimeter, but a different area.

   a.   b.

FROM Rope TO Rulers

Have you ever wondered how people measured the area and perimeter of large spaces before they had the measuring tools we have today?

In ancient Egypt, they used ropes. The ropes were knotted to mark distances, just like rulers or measuring tapes are marked to show centimetres.

What were these ropes used for? They were used to map out the size and shape of a farmer's grain field. Every year, the Nile River flooded its banks. The flooding washed away the markers that showed the boundaries of the fields. After each flood, men called "rope stretchers" would put the markers back. To do this, they would bring the knotted ropes and stretch them tightly. They put markers in the ground where the knots showed they should be.

When the rope stretchers were finished, each person could see once again where to plant his or her grain.

· ·

1 Compare knotted ropes to measuring tools you know today. Which do you think work better? Why?

2 What are some uses you can think of for measuring with knotted ropes today?

3 Create a knotted rope measuring tool of your own. How long will the rope be? How far apart will the knots be? What will you use your rope for?

PLANNING A School Garden

You are a landscape architect. You have the responsibility of planning a pleasing garden for your school. The garden will be a rectangle 14 m wide and 18 m long. Decide whether the garden will grow vegetables or flowers or a combination of both. Work with your group to create a drawing of the school garden.

- Pick five plants you want to grow.
- Decide how to divide the garden into five plots.
- Find the area and the perimeter of the entire garden.
- Find the area and the perimeter of each of the five plots in the garden.
- Write a report that compares the different plots. Tell why you divided the garden the way you did.

Check YOURSELF

Great job! You decided on five types of plants. You divided the garden into five usable areas. You found the perimeter and area of each plot and of the entire garden. Your report explained why you divided the garden the way you did.

P R O B L E M

BANK

1. Suppose you have to make a book cover for this math book. What measurements do you need to make? How big is the piece of paper you will need?

2. One pitcher holds 1.5 L; another pitcher holds 500 mL. Is the combined capacity greater than, less than, or equal to 2 L? Explain.

3. Carpet comes in a roll 4 m wide. What length do you need to buy to carpet a room 5 m by 7 m? How much carpet will be left over? Draw a diagram to show how you would cut the carpet.

4. Look at the tile design on the right. How can you remove four tiles, so that the remaining tiles have the same perimeter, but an area of 5 square units?

5. Suppose you have a string 18 units long. How can you use it to make two rectangles, one of which has an area twice as big as the other? Use grid paper to show your solution.

6. Sal and Teddy cut flowers like this out of construction paper.

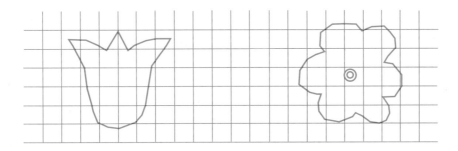

    a. Estimate the perimeter of each flower. Then measure the perimeter as accurately as you can.

    b. Estimate the area of each flower. Then find the area as accurately as you can.

7. Use centimetre grid paper. Draw as many rectangles as you can with an area of 36 cm². Cut them out. Order them from least to greatest width. Then find the perimeter of each rectangle. What pattern do you notice?

8. Abbas is putting a border where the walls meet the ceiling of a room. He has a 20-m roll of border. Both Room A and Room B have ceiling areas of 24 m². The roll of border is enough for one room, but not the other. What could be the dimensions of the rooms?

9. Erika invented a game that uses a game board. The perimeter of the game board must be 140 cm. The game board should be as close to a square as possible. What should the dimensions of the game board be?

SKILL BANK
FROM THIS UNIT

1. What unit would you use to measure?

   a. the capacity of a perfume bottle   **b.** the mass of an adult

   c. the distance from home to school   **d.** the length of the gym

   e. the capacity of a pot   **f.** the width of a calculator

2. What is each missing number or symbol?

   a. 1 kL = ■ L   **b.** 1 km = ■ m   **c.** 1 m = ■ cm

   d. 1 m = 1000 ■   **e.** 1 L = ■ mL   **f.** 1000 kg = 1 ■

   g. 1000 ■ = 1 kg   **h.** 10 ■ = 1 cm   **i.** 1 m = ■ mm

3. Draw a different figure:

   a. with the same area, but a different perimeter

   b. with the same perimeter, but a different area

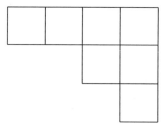

4. What is the approximate area and the approximate perimeter of each figure?

   a.

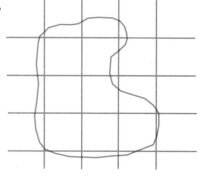

   b.

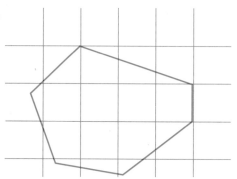

5. Measure to find the perimeter.

   a.

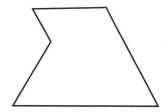

   b.

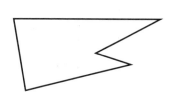

SKILL BANK
LOOKING BACK

1. A company is planning its retirement policy. It collected these data on how many years each employee has worked at the company: 2, 7, 30, 6, 7, 8, 26, 20, 5, 9, 6, 4, 3, 19, 14, 30, 10, 16, 30, 12, 13, 3, 5, 4, 21, 3, 2, 4, 4, 5, 3, 6, 4, 3, 14, 10, 4, 3.
   a. Make a line plot to show the data.
   b. How can the line plot help the company with its plans?

2. Here are the heights of students in a grade 5 class.

140 cm	132 cm	138 cm	131 cm	145 cm
138 cm	146 cm	141 cm	152 cm	136 cm
141 cm	144 cm	138 cm	150 cm	143 cm
126 cm	137 cm	122 cm	146 cm	142 cm

   a. What can you use as the stem in a stem-and-leaf plot?
   b. Make a stem-and-leaf plot to show the data.

3. Which expression matches Spinner A?
   Which expression matches Spinner B?
   - as likely to spin red as blue
   - more likely to spin red than blue
   - less likely to spin red than blue

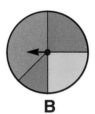

A   **B**

4. Match the terms to the events.

certain	**a.** It will snow in April.
possible	**b.** It will snow in June.
impossible	**c.** It will snow in December.
likely	**d.** The sun will rise tomorrow.
not likely	**e.** The sun will not rise tomorrow.

What figures cover completely?

EXPLORING TESSELLATIONS

STARTING OUT

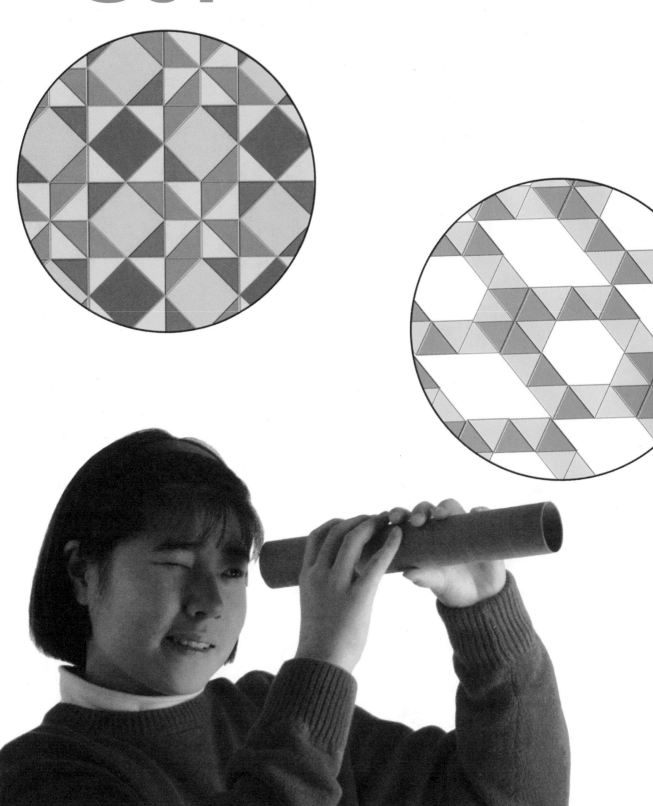

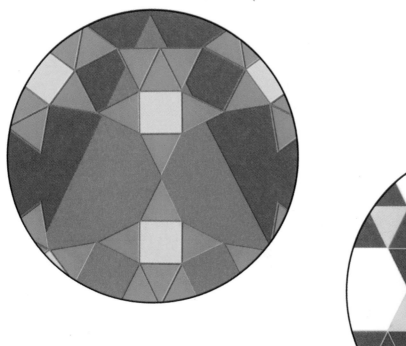

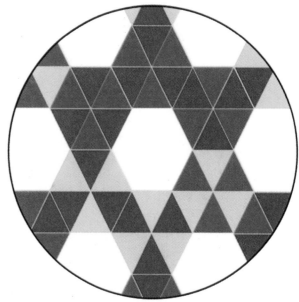

1 • Which kaleidoscope has four or more different polygons?

• Name some of the polygons that you see.

• Draw your own kaleidoscope picture! Describe the patterns. Write down the names of the polygons you know.

• Draw some of the polygons that you can create using squares and triangles.

• How many different polygons can you make using four triangles?

My Journal: What do you know about how polygons combine?

2 ● Write your name on a square piece of paper.
Cut the square into 5 to 13 pieces.

● Find a partner. Challenge your partner to try to put
your name together.

● Describe in writing some of the polygons you and your
partner used. Which polygons can you name?

● Take your partner's figures and your figures. Sort
them into two groups in any way you wish. Be prepared
to present your sets and describe the way you sorted to
the class.

● Which figures did you use most? How could you find
which figures the class used most?

My Journal: What polygon puzzles were hard to
solve? Why? Suppose you were to make another
polygon puzzle. What would you do differently?

Exploring Tessellations

Discuss each design in your group.

More Tessellations

A tessellation is a set of figures that covers a whole
surface with no space between the figures.
Tessellations are also called *tilings*.

▶ Which picture does not show
  a tessellation?

A regular tessellation is made with just one regular polygon repeated over and over. All the tiles are congruent. These tessellations are edge-to-edge.

▶ What polygons do you see in each picture?

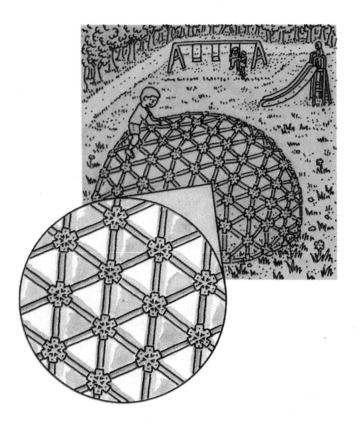

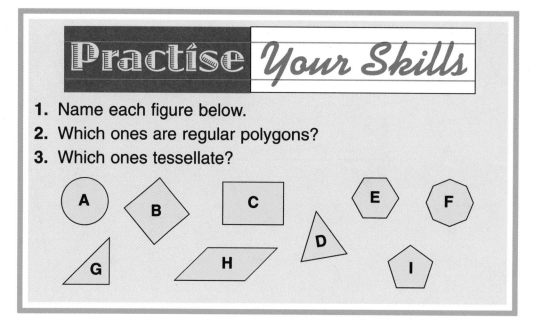

Practise Your Skills

1. Name each figure below.
2. Which ones are regular polygons?
3. Which ones tessellate?

A   B   C   E   F

G   H   D   I

The Latest In
HOME FASHIONS

Have you ever wondered where patterns for material in your home might come from? You could furnish your home in tessellations. First you might choose from a variety of Islamic tiling patterns for your floors.

Some of your curtains might be made from African fabrics.

Now all you need is a colourful stained glass window.

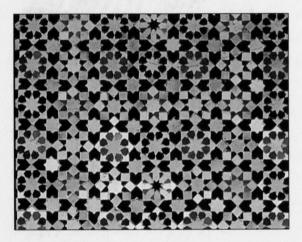

You might cover some of your floors with Salish rug designs.

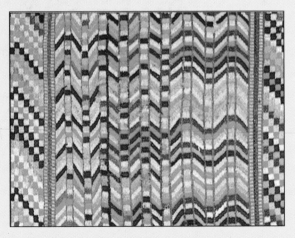

1 Look for tessellating patterns in your home, school, or neighbourhood. See if you can find where they came from.

2 Use some polygons you like to make a tessellating pattern. Tell where you might like to use it in your home.

3 Do you prefer tessellating patterns or other kinds of patterns? Explain your choice.

Polygon Tessellations

▶ Which polygons are used in these tessellations?
Are the polygons regular?

1. Describe the polygons you see in each picture. Are they regular polygons?

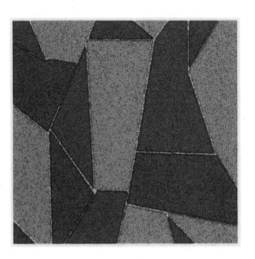

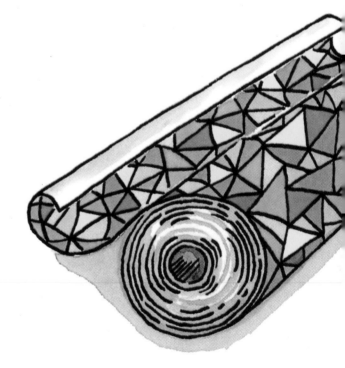

2. *My Journal:* What have you learned about tessellations so far?

235

Tessellation Combinations

▶ Discuss each tessellation. Name the polygons.

ON YOUR OWN

1.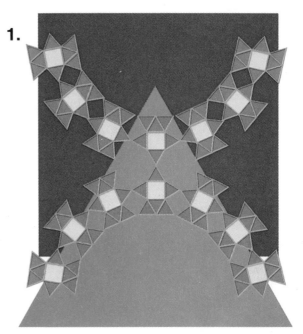

2.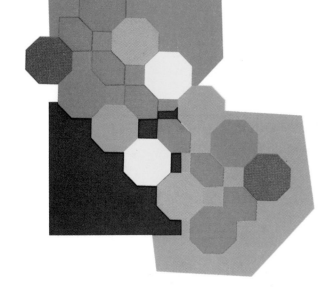

3.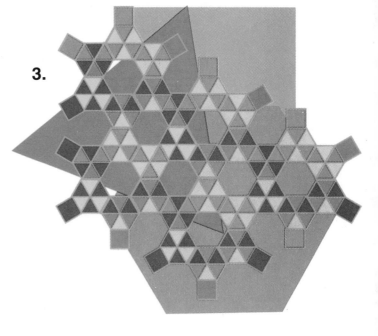

4.

5. *My Journal:* Is there anything about tessellations you do not understand? Explain your difficulties.

A PUZZLING PROBLEM

How are these puzzles alike?
How are they different?

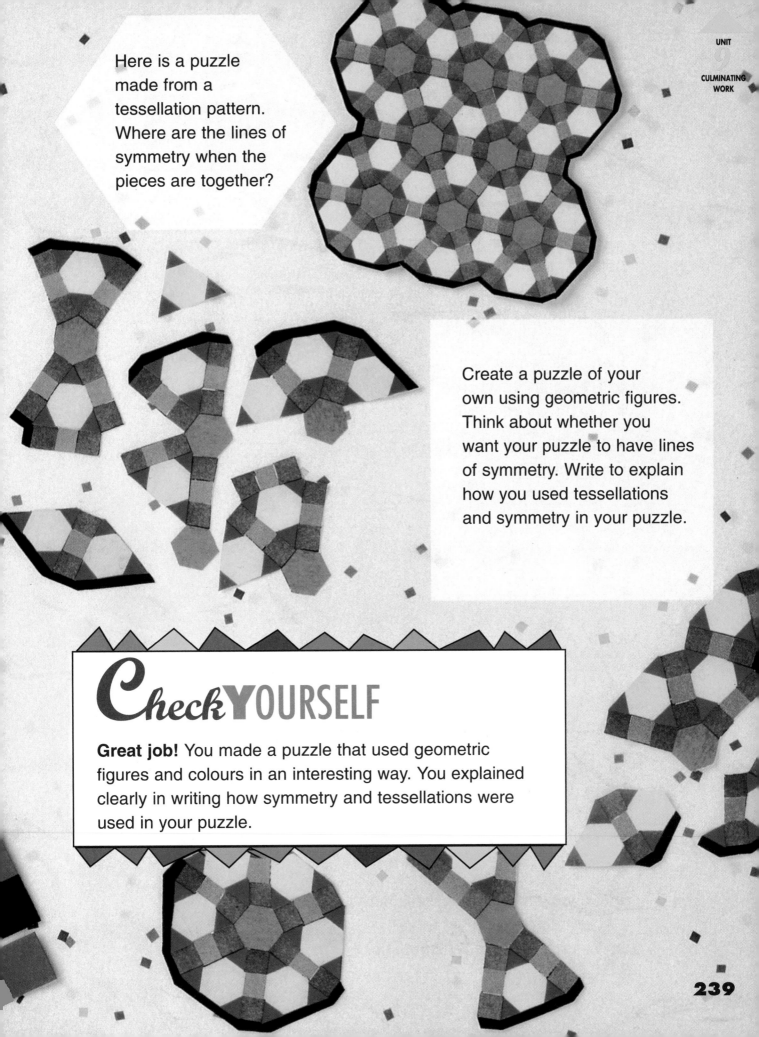

Here is a puzzle made from a tessellation pattern. Where are the lines of symmetry when the pieces are together?

Create a puzzle of your own using geometric figures. Think about whether you want your puzzle to have lines of symmetry. Write to explain how you used tessellations and symmetry in your puzzle.

𝒞heck**Y**OURSELF

Great job! You made a puzzle that used geometric figures and colours in an interesting way. You explained clearly in writing how symmetry and tessellations were used in your puzzle.

PROBLEM BANK

1. Sit at a table facing a partner. Stand a book or other barrier between the two of you, so you can't see each other.
Use Power Polygons to build a tessellating pattern. Describe your pattern to your partner using only words. Have your partner build your pattern. Remove the barrier. See if the two patterns match. Reverse roles.

   a. Try again. Did you get better the second time?

   b. What made it easier the second time?

2. Find a way to cover the tessellation below with different polygons.

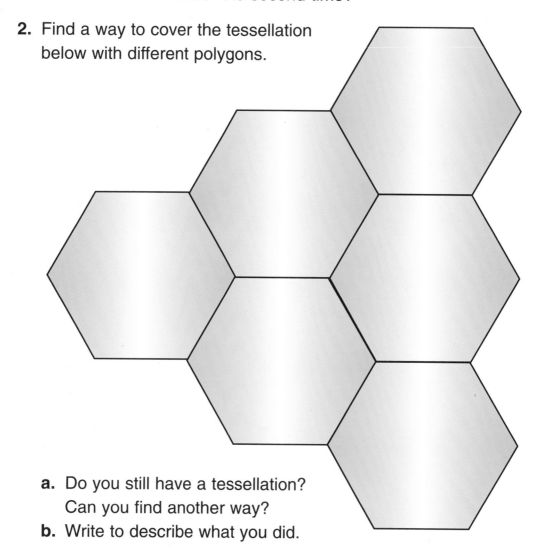

   a. Do you still have a tessellation? Can you find another way?

   b. Write to describe what you did.

3. Trace and cut out these figures.

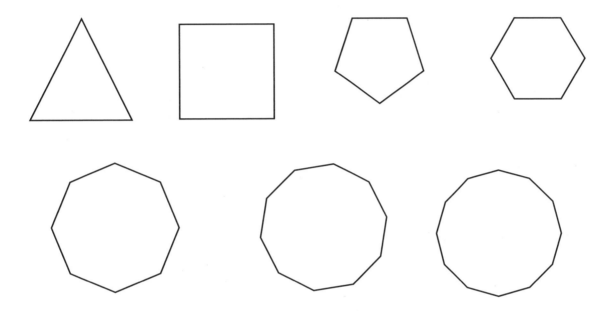

    a. Find out which of these figures tessellate.

    b. Some polygons tessellate and some do not. Discuss why this is so with a partner. Write your explanation.

    c. Can you make a tessellation with non-tessellating polygons if you combine two or more figures? Explain your thinking.

4. Draw a figure that you think won't tessellate. Try it. Were you right? Explain your thinking.

5. You are a contractor. Your client wants to use two different kinds of brick tiles to finish the driveway. What figures do you suggest would work best? What pattern would emerge from these figures? Draw a diagram to go with your recommendation.

SKILL BANK FROM THIS UNIT

1. Select a regular polygon from the set of Power Polygons. Place it in the centre of a piece of paper. Create a design around it using other polygons. Do not leave any gaps between the polygons.

2. **a.** Use Activity Master 1. Which figures can you cover completely with other Power Polygons? Make a drawing or tracing to show how to do it. If you can find more than one way, show the other ways too.

   b. Do the same thing for the figures on Activity Master 2.

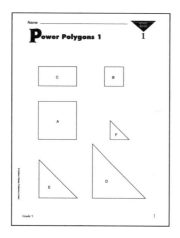

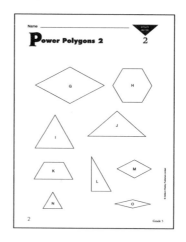

3.
   a. Trace around a Power Polygon like this.
   b. Slide the figure. Trace it.
   c. Turn the figure. Trace it.
   d. Flip the figure. Trace it.

4. Find a triangle in the Power Polygon set that you can use two of to make a rectangle. Tell whether you slide, flip, or turn the triangle to do it.

SKILL BANK
LOOKING BACK

1. Match the results of each person's 40 spins to a spinner.

	Red	Blue	White
Enzio	12	14	14
Sophie	10	11	19
Abbas	13	8	19

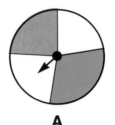 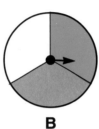 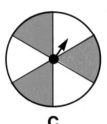

A   B   C

2. What unit would you use to measure?
   a. the length of your classroom
   b. the mass of an apple
   c. the capacity of a cup
   d. the capacity of a sink
   e. the distance you could bicycle in an hour

3.

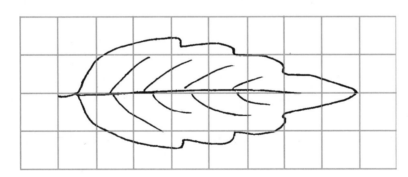

   a. What is the approximate area of the leaf?
   b. About what is the perimeter of the leaf?

4. Use 12 coloured tiles. Make figures with these perimeters.
   a. 16 units   b. 14 units   c. 26 units

*H*ow can we describe and build boxes?

BUILDING AND FILLING BOXES

S·T·A·R·T·I·N·G
OUT

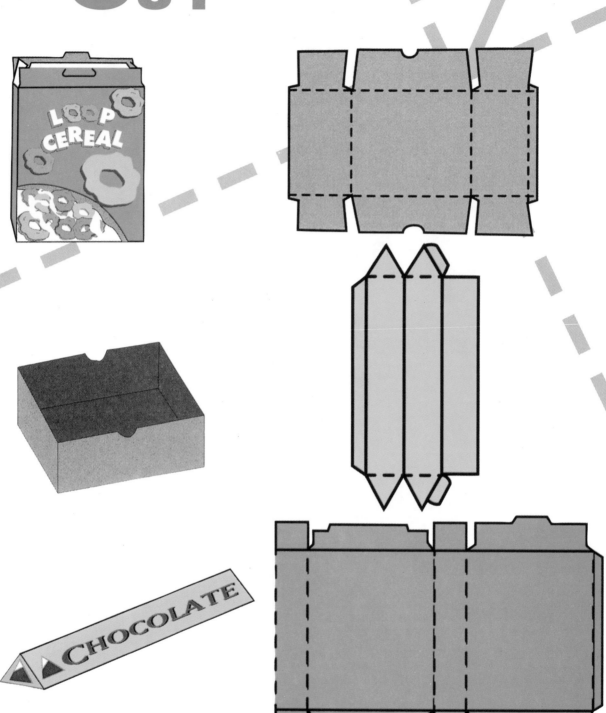

1 ● Which pattern do you think matches which box? How do you know?

● How many faces does each box have? How can the pattern help you figure that out?

● How are the patterns alike? How are they different?

● What familiar figures do you see in these boxes?

My Journal: Think of boxes you have seen in stores. Why do you think they are designed the way they are? What decisions do you think box designers have to make?

BUILDING AND FILLING BOXES

S·TAR·TIN·G

OUT

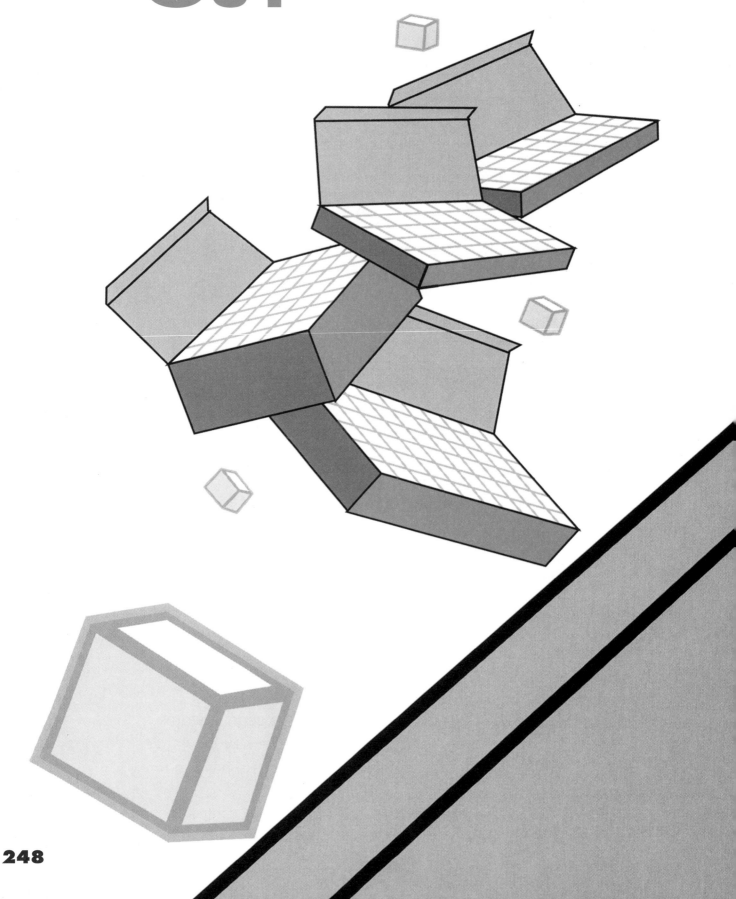

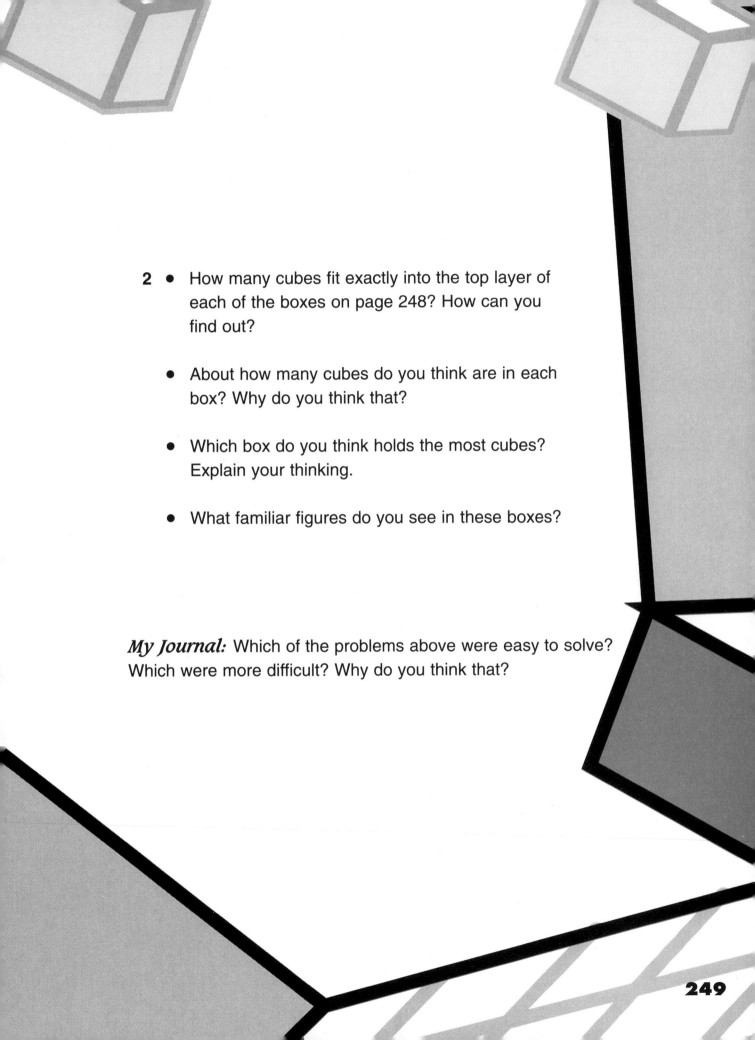

2 • How many cubes fit exactly into the top layer of each of the boxes on page 248? How can you find out?

• About how many cubes do you think are in each box? Why do you think that?

• Which box do you think holds the most cubes? Explain your thinking.

• What familiar figures do you see in these boxes?

My Journal: Which of the problems above were easy to solve? Which were more difficult? Why do you think that?

Exploring Rectangular Boxes

▶ Compare these boxes. How are they different?
How are they the same?

Finding the Greatest Volume

▶ Which box do you think will hold the greatest number of centimetre cubes?

▶ What is the largest closed-top box you can make with a rectangular piece of paper?

Words to Know

Volume: a measure of the space occupied by a three-dimensional object. We can measure volume in cubic centimetres.

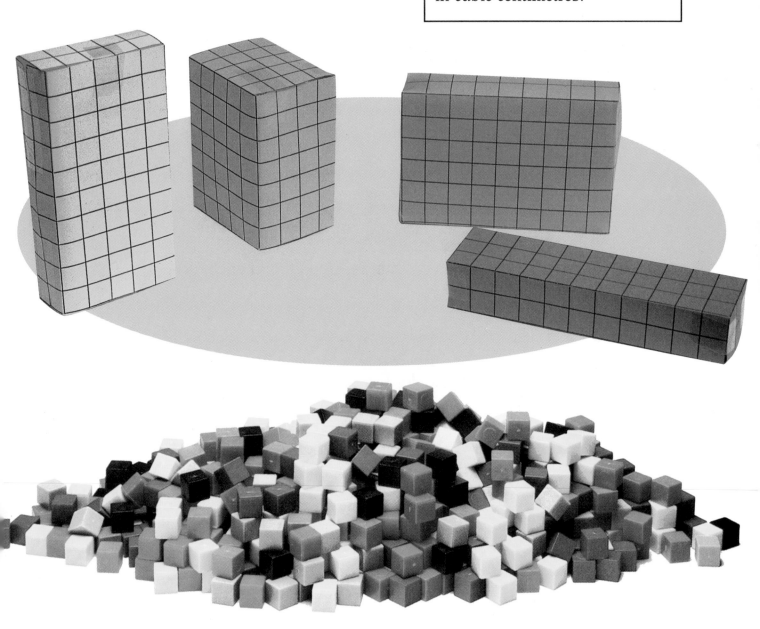

ON YOUR OWN

1. Look at these boxes. How many other boxes can you draw with a volume of 100 cm³?
Label the dimensions of each.
Make all dimensions whole numbers.

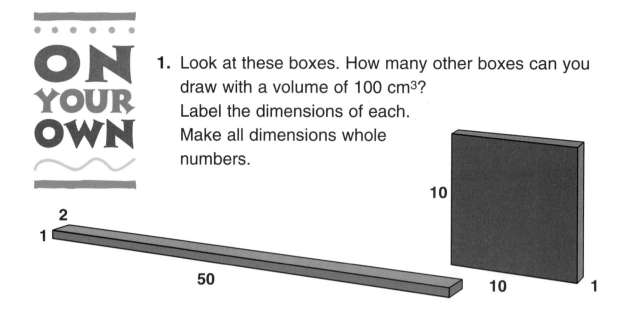

2. The volume of a box is 80 cm³. One dimension is 5 cm. What are some possible numbers for the other dimensions?

3. *My Journal:* Is the tallest box always the box with the greatest volume? Explain how you know.

Practise Your Skills

How many cubes are there all together in each "building"? Write to tell how you decided.

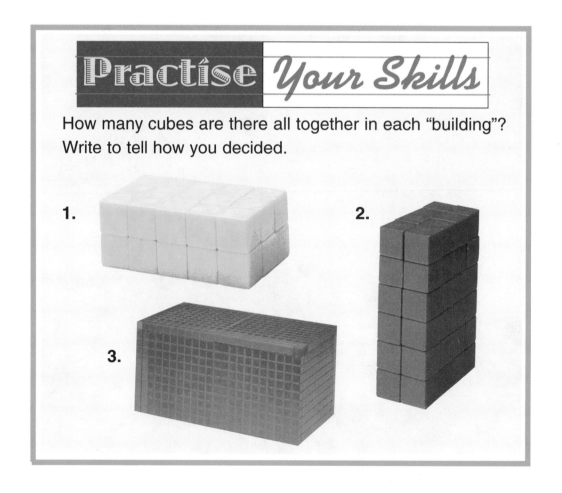

1.

2.

3.

Different Solids, Same Volume

▶ Are there other ways to arrange 12 cubes?
Tell how you decided.

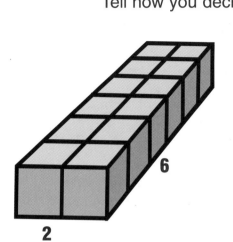

1

2

6

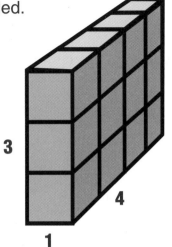

3

1

4

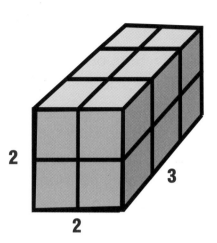

2

2

3

▶ In each pair below, are the boxes the same or different?
Write to tell how you decided.

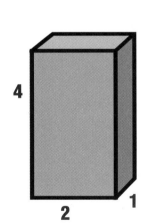

4

2

1

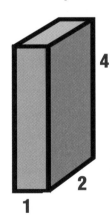

4

1

2

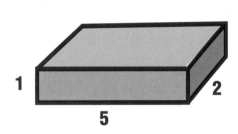

1

5

2

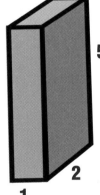

5

1

2

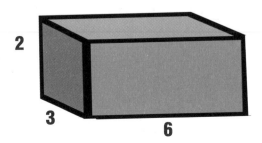

2

3

6

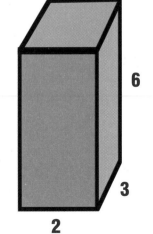

6

2

3

253

1. Suppose you want to build a box to hold 100 cubes. You put 20 cubes in the bottom layer. How many layers of cubes will you need? What are the dimensions of the box? What other dimensions could you use for a box to hold 100 cubes?

2. Which has the greater volume: a box that has 4 layers of 16 cubes or a box that has 8 layers of 8 cubes? Explain your answer.

3. *My Journal:* Tell how the number of cubes in the bottom layer is related to the total number of cubes in a box. Draw diagrams to show your explanation.

Practise Your Skills

Find the volume of each box.
1. length 8 cm, width 6 cm, height 2 cm
2. length 9 cm, width 12 cm, height 6 cm
3. length 12 cm, width 10 cm, height 8 cm
4. length 25 cm, width 20 cm, height 10 cm
5. height 15 cm, width 5 cm, length 10 cm
6. width 12 cm, length 12 cm, height 12 cm
7. height 20 cm, width 20 cm, length 21 cm
8. width 3 cm, height 30 cm, length 6 cm

Nets for Cubes

▶ Which pattern can be folded to make an open-top box?

1. Can each pattern be folded to make a closed-top box? If not, why not?

a.

b.  **c.** **d.**

2. Draw a hexomino that can be folded to make a box. Don't use one from above.

3. *My Journal:* What have you learned about square patterns and boxes?

Practise Your Skills

Which box in each pair has the greater volume?

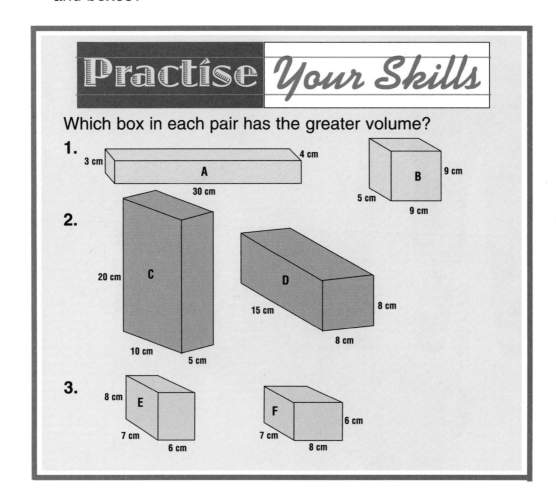

1.
- A: 3 cm, 4 cm, 30 cm
- B: 9 cm, 5 cm, 9 cm

2.
- C: 20 cm, 10 cm, 5 cm
- D: 15 cm, 8 cm, 8 cm

3.
- E: 8 cm, 7 cm, 6 cm
- F: 6 cm, 7 cm, 8 cm

Exploring Surfaces of Boxes

▷ What is the smallest size of paper
that could be used to cover the box?

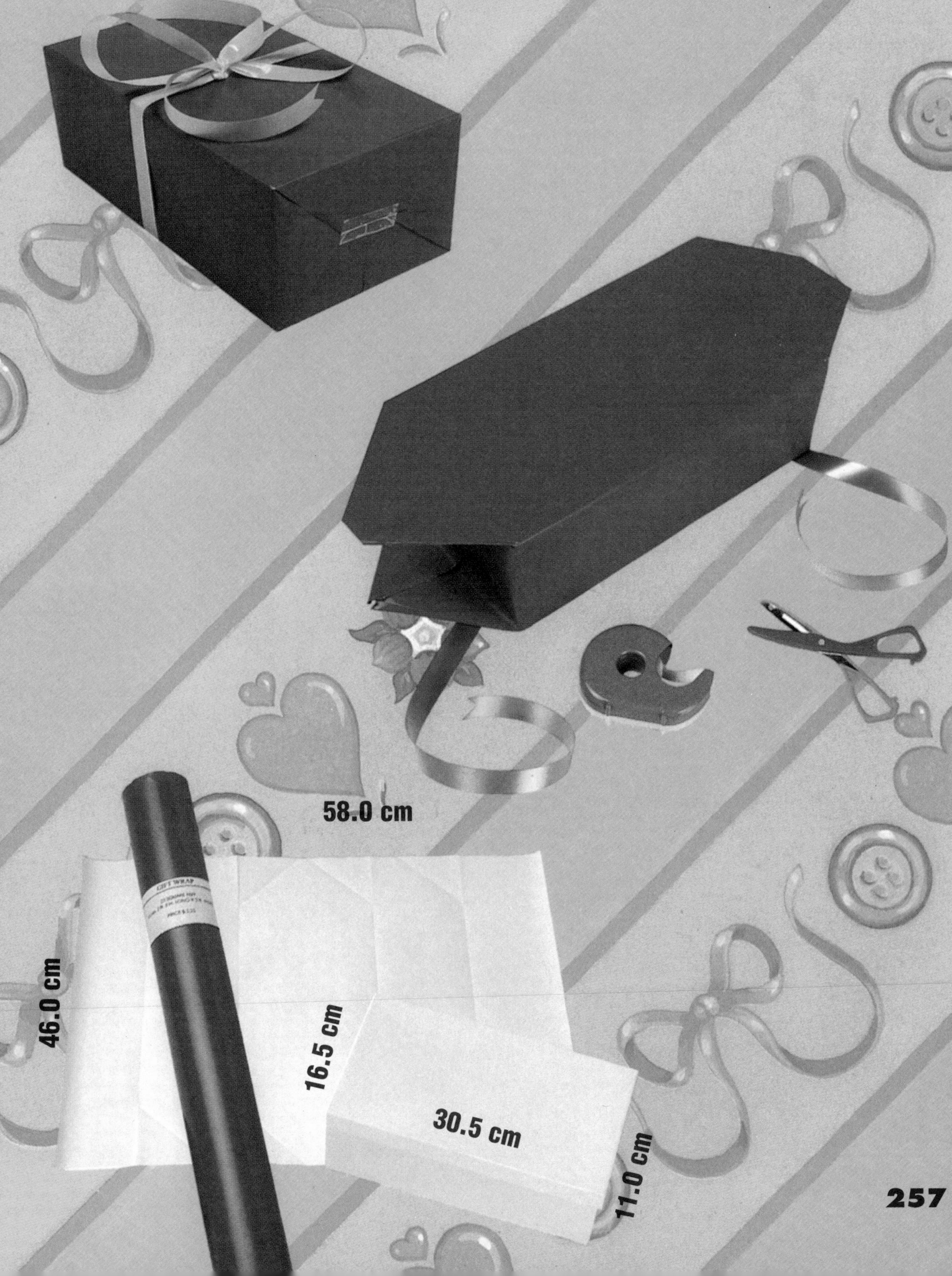

58.0 cm

46.0 cm

16.5 cm

30.5 cm

11.0 cm

PACK THEM IN

Have you ever wondered how people decide on packaging materials for shipping?

Have you ever eaten any of these fruits? How did they taste?

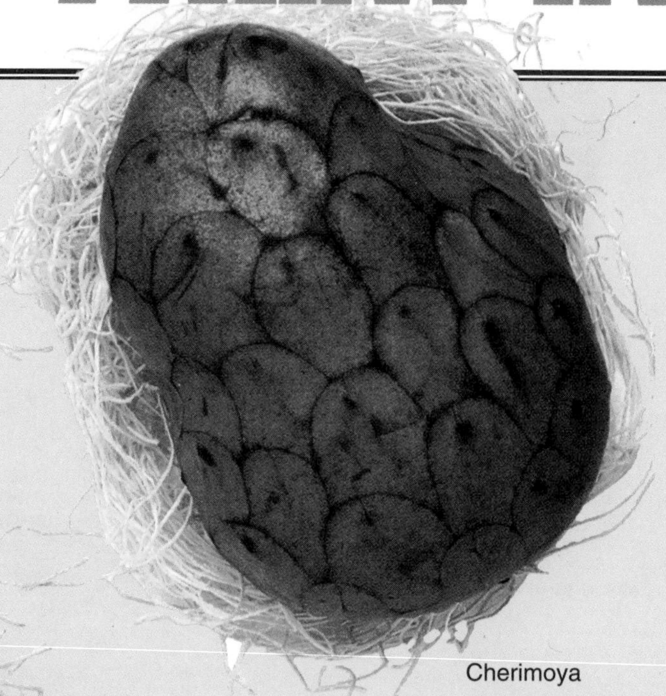

Cherimoya

Heart-shaped

Very tasty when ripe

Native to the Andes Mountains; grown in Chile and along the California coast

Size: about the same as a person's fist

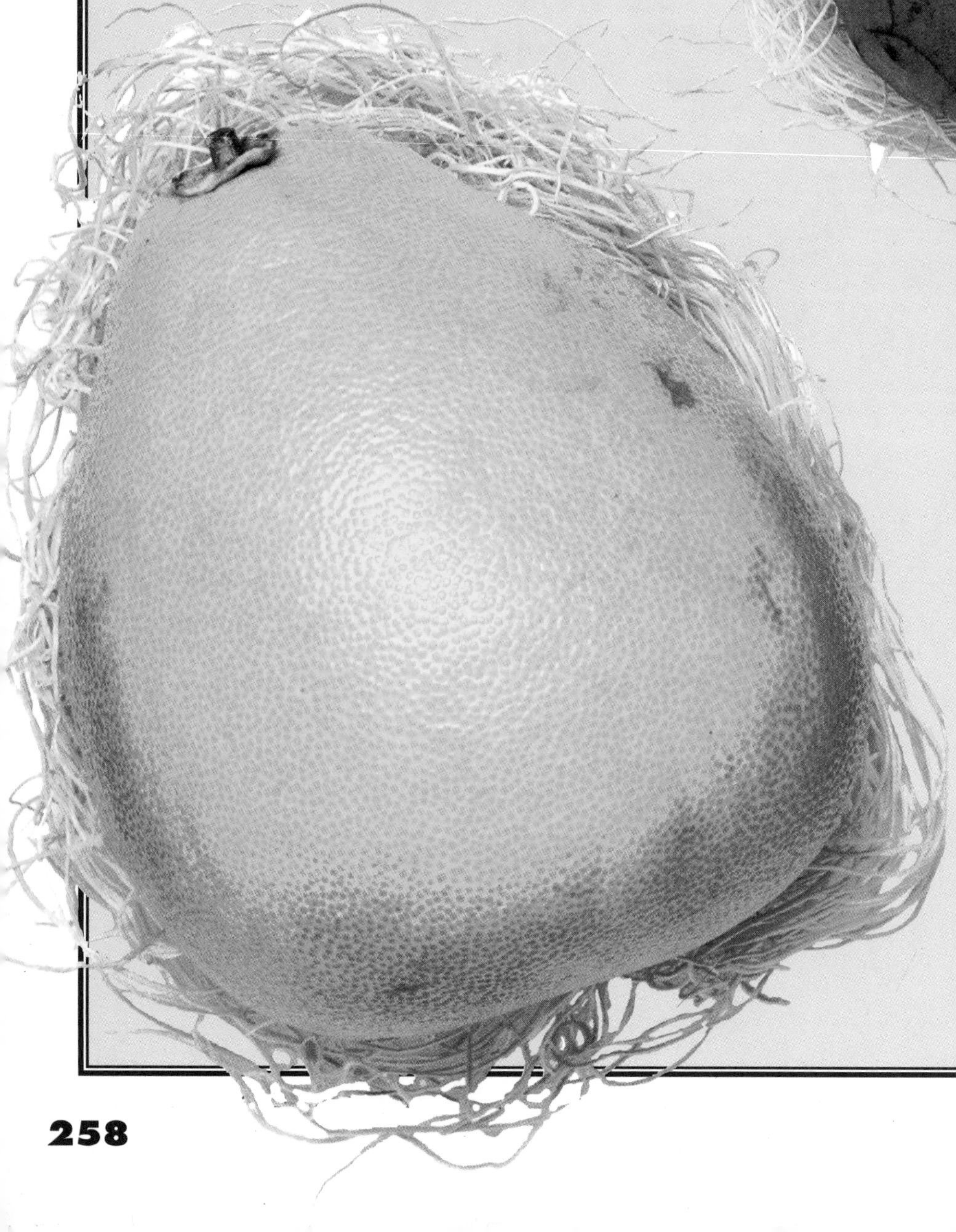

Pummelos

Largest citrus fruit

Can be round or pear-shaped

Grown in Southeast Asia: India, China, Indonesia, and introduced to the West Indies

Now also grown in Israel

Size: between a grapefruit and a basketball

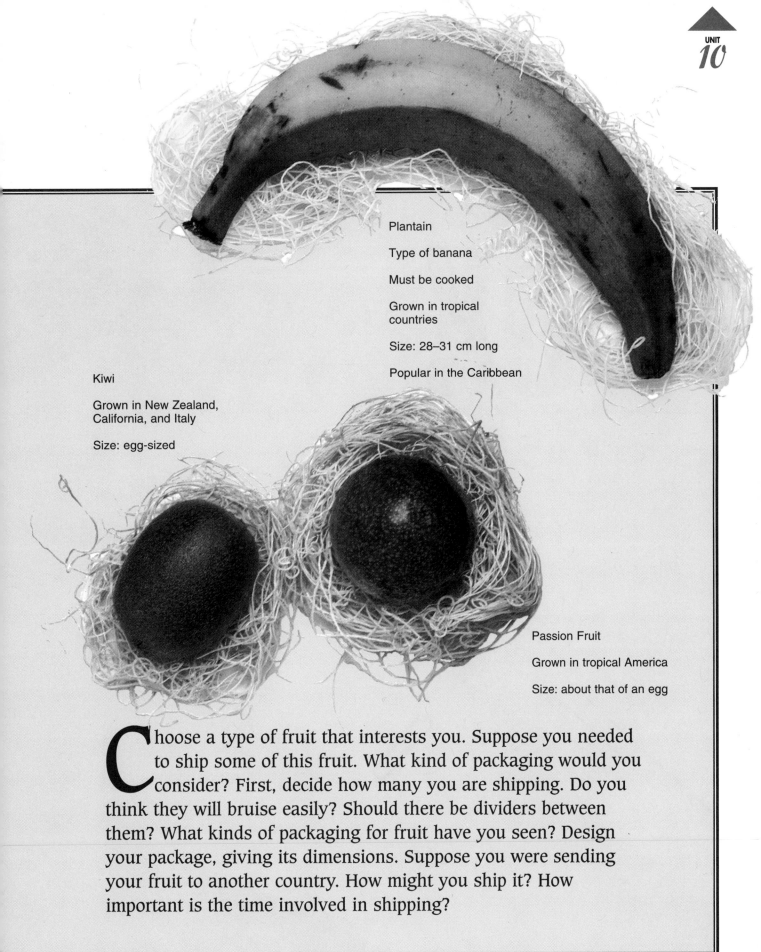

Plantain

Type of banana

Must be cooked

Grown in tropical countries

Size: 28–31 cm long

Popular in the Caribbean

Kiwi

Grown in New Zealand, California, and Italy

Size: egg-sized

Passion Fruit

Grown in tropical America

Size: about that of an egg

Choose a type of fruit that interests you. Suppose you needed to ship some of this fruit. What kind of packaging would you consider? First, decide how many you are shipping. Do you think they will bruise easily? Should there be dividers between them? What kinds of packaging for fruit have you seen? Design your package, giving its dimensions. Suppose you were sending your fruit to another country. How might you ship it? How important is the time involved in shipping?

BUILDING A BOX

What size box will hold 1000 pencils?

Work in a small group to design an
open-top box that will hold 1000 pencils.
Think about these questions.

- How can we make a box that does not
  have any wasted space inside?

- What kind of pattern will make an open-
  top box?

- What measurements will we need?

- Will we pack the pencils in layers or rows?

- How many layers or rows of pencils will
  there be?

Work together to make a box
that will hold 1000 pencils.

Check **YOURSELF**

Great job! The box you designed and built held 1000
pencils without too much wasted space. The net for
the box was neat and accurate. You were able to
communicate your plans for the box clearly in writing.

PROBLEM BANK

1. A publisher wants to send 10 copies of this student book to a school.

   a. What size box does the publisher need? Write a description of the box and include a drawing to make your recommendation clear.

   b. What would a box for 15 copies of the book look like? How would this box be different from the one for 10 books?

2. Make a small box using Activity Master 8, Number Cube Pattern.

   a. Get one centimetre cube. Use it to figure out about how many cubes will fit in the box you made. Explain how you estimated the number of cubes.

   b. Check your estimate using centimetre cubes. What did you find out?

   c. What other boxes could you build using that many cubes? Sketch each arrangement you find.

3. When you make a box to hold 11 cubes, you can only make one box. Its dimensions are 11 by 1 by 1.

   a. What other numbers of cubes between 10 and 20 can fit in only one box?

   b. Which numbers of cubes can fit in two types of boxes? Which fit more than two types of boxes?

4. Choose a number of cubes. Record the number. Find as many different ways as you can to make boxes to hold that number of cubes. Record all the ways you find.

5. Find two small boxes that no one needs any more.

   a. Draw what you think they will look like when you cut them and lay them flat.

   b. Cut them so they lie flat. Make sure you cut so that all faces are still attached. Write a description of each box.

   c. How do the nets of your boxes compare? Write about how they are alike and how they are different.

6. Here are the dimensions of two boxes.

   Box 1 is 40 cm by 20 cm by 10 cm

   Box 2 is 30 cm by 15 cm by 30 cm

   a. Estimate which would need more wrapping paper. Explain your estimates.

   b. Figure out the least amount of wrapping paper needed for each box. What did you find out? Describe what you did.

SKILL BANK
FROM THIS UNIT

1. How many centimetre cubes do you think there are in each solid?

a.

2 cm

2 cm

5 cm

b.

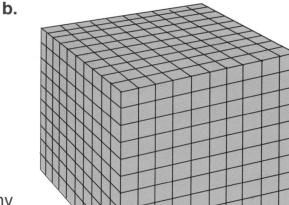

2. a. Sketch a box that will hold exactly 18 cubes. Describe the box. Tell how many cubes long, wide, and tall it is.

b. What other boxes can you make to hold 18 cubes? Describe them.

3. How many different ways could you build a rectangular box that will hold 48 cubes? Draw and label diagrams to show all the ways.

4. Find the volume of each box.

a.

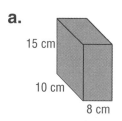

15 cm

10 cm

8 cm

b.

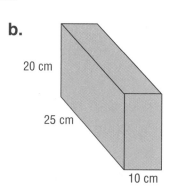

20 cm

25 cm

10 cm

5. A box holds 60 centimetre cubes. One dimension of the box is 4 cm. What might the other dimensions be?

SKILL BANK
LOOKING BACK

1. A rectangular field is 16 m long and 9 m wide.
   What is its perimeter? What is its area?

2. Draw four different figures with an area of 8 cm².
   Which has the greatest perimeter?

3. Name something that you could measure using each unit.
   a. metres   **b.** tonnes
   c. grams   **d.** square centimetres

4. Choose the best estimate of the mass of each person.
   a.    **b.**

   10 g   100 g   10 kg   4 kg   40 kg   400 kg

5. Each tile in this tessellation can be moved onto a nearby tile by a slide, flip, or turn. What motion will move the black tile onto the
   a. green tile?
   b. red tile?
   c. orange tile?
   d. yellow tile?

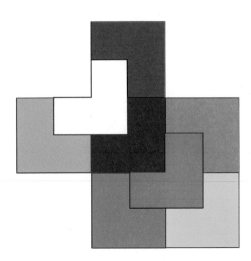

265

How can we create and design figures?

**CREATING AND
ANALYZING FIGURES**

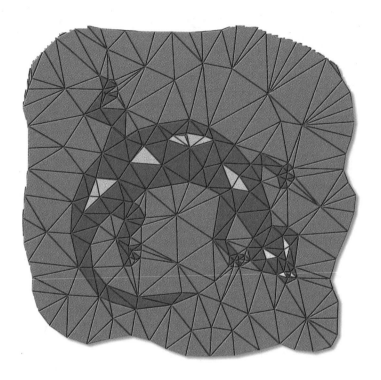

1 • How are the figures in each
design related?

• How do you think these designs
were created?

• Create a design that you think
belongs on this page.

My Journal: What do you think
is important to include when you are
describing a figure to someone?

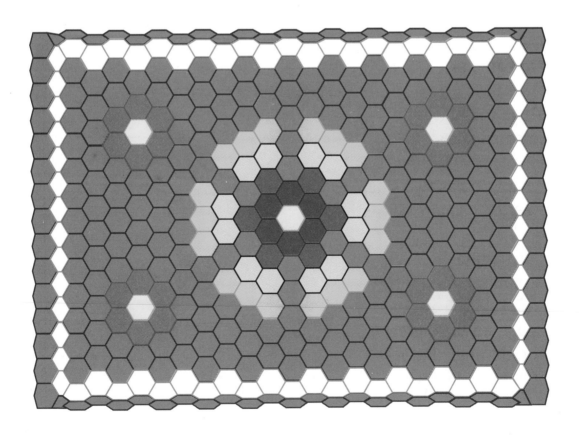

Investigating Triangles

▶ What types of triangles can you make? Can you always make a triangle? Use toothpicks to make triangles. Record the ones that you make. A chart like this can help organize your work. What patterns can you find?

Lengths of Sides (toothpicks)	Equilateral Triangle	Isosceles Triangle	Scalene Triangle	Number of Acute Angles	Number of Obtuse Angles	Number of Right Angles
1, 1, 1	✓	✗	✗	3	0	0
2, 2, 2						
2, 2, 3						

Words to Know

An **equilateral** triangle has three equal sides.

An **isosceles** triangle has two equal sides.

A **scalene** triangle has no equal sides.

A **right angle** has two sides that meet at a square corner.

An **acute angle** is less than a right angle.

An **obtuse angle** is greater than a right angle but less than a straight line.

1. Use up to 12 toothpicks. Try to make as many squares and rectangles as you can. How many toothpicks do you use for each? What patterns can you find?

2. Make a triangle with a right angle and an acute angle. What is the third angle? Can you make the triangle another way? Explain your thinking.

3. Can you draw a triangle that has a right angle, an obtuse angle, and an acute angle? Explain your thinking. Now draw a polygon that has those angles. How many sides does it have? Can you make one with more sides? with fewer sides?

4. *My Journal:* What have you learned about triangles that you didn't know before?

Practise Your Skills

Look at the triangles.

1. Which triangle does not belong?

2. Why does it not belong?

3. Draw another triangle that does not belong. Explain why your triangle does not belong.

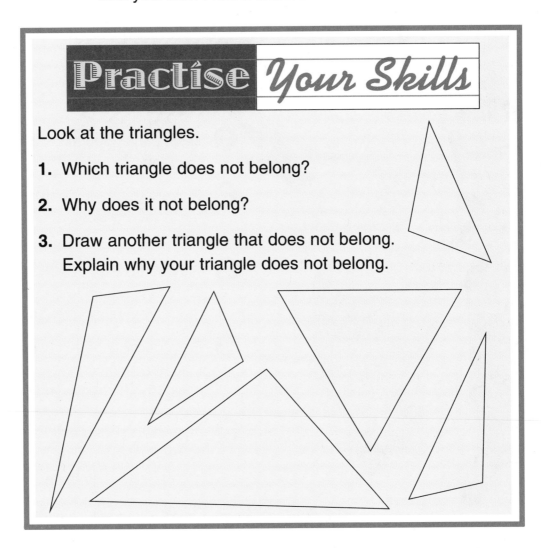

WHAT'S THE POLYGON? GAME

Group

Pairs or small groups

Materials

Each player needs:
• paper

Each pair needs:
• ruler
• several Power Polygons

Game Rules

1 Each player secretly selects a Power Polygon.

2 Players trace their polygons. They measure the sides and classify the angles.

3 Players take turns asking one another questions about their poygons. They record the information they collect.

4 Players continue to collect information until they think they can draw the secret polygon. They draw the polygon.

5 Players get one point for drawing the correct polygon. Players who ask the fewest questions get a bonus point.

1. Draw a polygon of your choice on grid paper. Write to describe it as fully as you can.
Read the description aloud to a friend. Have your friend follow the description to draw your polygon. Do the polygons match? How could you revise your description?

2. On grid paper, draw a polygon that has 4 sides. Do not draw a square, rectangle, parallelogram, or a trapezoid. What did you draw?

3. On grid paper, draw a polygon with 4 sides that are all different lengths. What type of angles are there?

4. *My Journal:* What do you need to know to draw a polygon?

Practise Your Skills

Identify each polygon. Draw the polygon.

1. a polygon with 4 equal sides and 4 equal angles

2. a polygon with 2 pairs of equal sides and 4 equal angles

3. a polygon with 3 angles, one of which is a right angle

4. a polygon with 4 equal sides, and 2 pairs of equal angles

5. a polygon with 6 sides

6. a polygon with 5 angles

Covering Figures

Use your tangram pieces to cover each figure on this page.

▶ For each figure, how many pieces do you need?

Use your tangram pieces.
Try to make figures with the same
shapes as these.
▶ Which figures can't you make?
Explain why when you can't. Draw the
extra pieces you need to make the
figures you can't make.

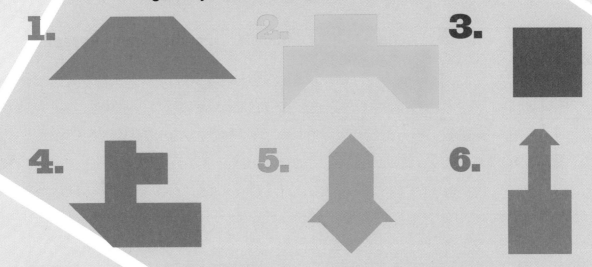

1.   **2.**   **3.**

4.   **5.**   **6.**

Think of the small tangram square
as 1 unit square. Use your
tangram pieces to answer these
questions.

1. Make a letter of the alphabet.
What is its area?

2. Make a different letter with the same area.
How do you know the letters have the same area?

3. Make a figure with an area of 6 square units.
Sketch it. Can you make a different figure
with the same area? Show your work.

4. *My Journal:* What have you learned about tangrams?

aking Polygons

▶ How can you make different polygons using the tangram pieces? Record what you find.

Number of tangram pieces used	Square ⬜	Rectangle ▭	Triangle △	Parallelogram ▱	Trapezoid ⏢
1					
2					
3					
4					
5					
6					
7					

276

BUILDINGS

Have you ever wondered what shapes are good for building things? Look at a bridge or a building under construction. Some of the figures and solids you can see are triangles and half-spheres, or hemispheres. These are some of the strongest figures and solids there are.

The oldest houses were huts made of mud and straw in the shape of hemispheres. The hemisphere appears as an arch in many ancient Roman buildings and bridges. Some Inuit build igloos, which are also hemispherical. Igloos are very strong and can be heated with just one small oil lamp.

The faces of pyramids in Egypt have the shape of a triangle. First Nations' teepees are made using a framework with triangles. Triangles also make up bridges and the skeletons of large office buildings.

1 Test the strength of a solid similar to a sphere. Hold an uncooked egg lengthwise between your palms. Now push hard. What did you find?

2 Choose a building that uses the shape of a hemisphere or a triangle in its construction. Research to find why it was built that way. Share your research with a friend.

Making POLYGON Puzzles

You have made and solved some interesting puzzles with tangram pieces. Now it's your turn to make a challenging puzzle.

You can use as many of the tangram pieces as you want. You can use more than one set. First decide on the polygon you want to make. Experiment to find ways to make it. Decide on the one you want to use to make a puzzle and then make it! Trace the polygon to make an outline of it.

You must write to tell the number of pieces in your puzzle and the name of the polygon. On another sheet of paper, give a solution that tells the pieces you used and shows how they are arranged.

Check YOURSELF

Great job! You chose a polygon and used the tangram pieces to make it. Next to your puzzle outline, you have the name of the polygon and the number of pieces needed to make it. The solution you provide is clear and easy to understand.

PROBLEM BANK

1. Examine this figure. How would you describe it? Make it with toothpicks.
   a. Move 4 toothpicks to make 3 equilateral triangles.
   b. Put the toothpicks back where they were. Now move 4 toothpicks to make 4 identical rhombuses.

2. Copy this dot array. Connect dots to make:

   •   •   •

   •   •   •

   •   •   •

   a. an angle less than a right angle
   b. an angle greater than a right angle
   c. a right angle
   d. an isosceles triangle
   e. a scalene triangle

3. A tetromino is formed by combining four squares, each the same size. The squares meet along the sides so that each square shares a side with at least one other square.

   Tetromino

   a. How many different tetrominoes can you find? Sketch them on centimetre grid paper.
   b. Which one, if any, has the smallest perimeter?
   c. Which one, if any, has the greatest perimeter?

4. Use 12 toothpicks to make this figure.

   a. Move 3 toothpicks to make
   3 identical squares.
   b. Put the toothpicks back.
   Now move 4 toothpicks to make
   3 identical squares.

5. Use a set of tangram pieces to solve
these problems. Use the small square as one unit.

   a. What is the easiest way to make a figure with an area
   of 4 square units? Explain your thinking.
   b. How many ways can you make a figure with an area
   of 3 square units? Draw them on dot paper or grid paper.
   Explain your thinking.

6. Use the set of tangram pieces to make this house.

7. Use a set of tangram pieces to make an animal, fish, or bird.
Trace around the outside edge. Give the outline to someone
else as a puzzle to solve.

SKILL BANK
FROM THIS UNIT

1. Which triangle does not belong with the rest?
   Explain why.

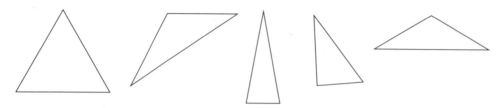

2. Define each figure.

   a. a square   **b.** a trapezoid   **c.** a scalene triangle

3. Use two of these  on a geoboard or dot paper to make:

   a. a square   **b.** a right triangle   **c.** a parallelogram

4. Use two of these  and 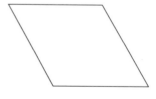 on a geoboard or dot paper to make:

   a. a rectangle   **b.** a trapezoid   **c.** a parallelogram

5. **a.** Trace these figures.

   b. For the square and rectangle, draw a line connecting one pair of
   opposite corners. For the other quadrilateral, draw a line connecting
   the opposite corners that are closer to each other.

   c. In each case, what kind of triangles did you make?

1. Use Power Polygons. Show as many ways as you can to cover this hexagon completely.

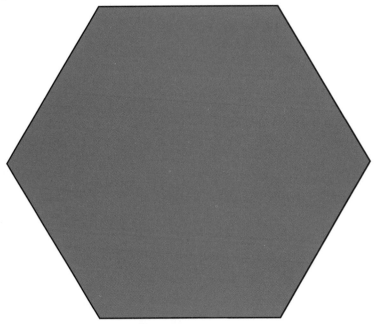

2. Can the pattern be folded to make a closed-top box?

a. 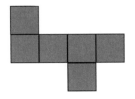   **b.** 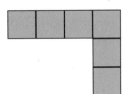   **c.**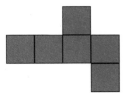

3. Find the volume.

a.

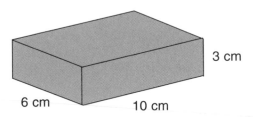

3 cm
6 cm   10 cm

b.

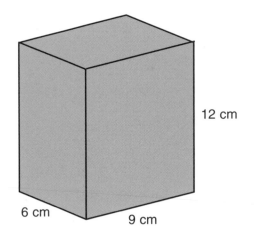

12 cm
6 cm   9 cm

4. How much paper would you need to cover all six faces of each box in exercise 3?

283

Index

Acknowledgments

ILLUSTRATION

Cover Illustration: **Seymour Chwast**
Cheryl Kirk Noll: 12-13; **Elizabeth Brady:** 15-16; **Clarence Porter:** 23, 24; **Roger Chandler:** 25;
Nan Brooks: 28-29; **Shelly Bartek:** 32-33; **Michael Groen:** 34; **Norm Eyolfson:** 42-43; **Peter Cook:** 44-45;
Stephen Taylor: 53; **Teco Rodrigues:** 56, 57; **Peter Cook:** 70; **Clarence Porter:** 71; **Teco Rodrigues:** 74;
Leon Zernitsky: 78; **Jane Sanders:** 80-81; **Victoria Kahn:** 82; **Vesna Krstanovich:** 89; **Margaret Hathaway:**
90, 91; **Barbara Spurll:** 96-97; **Teco Rodrigues:** 103; **Albert Lemant:** 104-105; **Jennifer Hewitson:** 106;
Reny Simard: 128-129; **Clarence Porter:** 130-131; **Leon Zernitsky:** 132; **Jennifer Bolten:** 133; **Teco
Rodrigues:** 133, 134; **Jennifer Bolten:** 135; **Darius Detwiler:** 136-137; **Teco Rodrigues:** 143; **Scott Snow:**
155-157; **Mike Reagan:** 158-160; **Mike Reed:** 161-163; **Vesna Krstanovich:** 174-175; **Stephen Taylor:**
180-181; **Bernadette Lau:** 191; **Patrick Fitzgerald:** 200-201; **Margaret Hathaway:** 202, 203; **Bernadette
Lau:** 204, 205; **Peter Cook:** 206-207; **Michelle Nidenoff:** 208-209; **Stephen Harris:** 210-211, 212;
Bernadette Lau: 217; **Lisa Snoddon:** 228-229; **Evan Polenghi:** 231, 232, 234, 235; **Meryl Rosner:** 234, 235;
Roger Chandler: 236-237; **Vicki Wehrman:** 246; **Lisa Snoddon:** 246; **Clarence Porter:** 250; **Teco Rodrigues:**
253; **Evan Polenghi:** 254; **Margaret Hathaway:** 262 **Clarence Porter:** 265; **Peter Cook:** 268, 269, 280, 281

PHOTOGRAPHY

Photo Management and Picture Research: **Omni-Photo Communications, Inc.**
Michael Groen: 6-7; © **Everett Collection:** 8; **Ian Crysler:** 9, 11; **Co Rentmeester/The Image Bank:** 12;
Paul Trummer/The Image Bank: 13; **Horizon:** 12-14, 18-20; © **The Newark Museum:** 26; **John Lei:** 27;
Horizon: 28, 30, 31; **Michael Groen:** 34; **Ian Crysler:** 40-41, 46, 47, 51; **Dave Starrett:** 54-55; **Everett
Studios:** 60-61; **Ian Crysler:** 62-63, 65, 67; **Ken Karp:** 68-69; **Ian Crysler:** 77; **Ken Karp:** 83; © **Hans
Pfletschinger/Peter Arnold Inc.:** 84; **Stephen J. Kransemann/Photo Researchers:** 85; **Everett Studios:** 86-87,
94-95; **Ian Crysler:** 98-99, 102-103; **Michael Groen:** 107; **Ken Karp:** 108; **Ray Boudreau:** 109; **Ian Crysler:**
110-111; **Everett Studios:** 118-119; **Michael Groen:** 118-119; © **Focus on Sports:** 118; © **The Canadian
Press:** 123; **Ian Crysler:** 126, 137; **Everett Studios:** 138-139; **Michael Groen:** 146-147; © **Tony Stone
Images:** 149; **Richard Hutchings:** 152; **Ken Karp:** 153, 154; **Fran Allan/Animals Animals:** 164 TL; **Fred
Whitehead/Animals Animals:** 164 BL; **Leonard Lee Rue III/Photo Researchers:** 164 TR; **Mickey Gibson/
Animals Animals:** 164 BR; © **Meyers/Okapia/Photo Researchers:** 165 TL; **Mickey Gibson/Animals Animals:**
165 BL; © **Ranjitsinh/Photo Researchers:** 165 TR; **Tom McHugh/Animals Animals:** 165 BR; **Richard
Hutchings:** 166; **Granger Collection:** 167 TL; **Steve Niedorf/ The Image Bank:** 167 BR; **Richard Hutchings:**
168; **Michael Groen:** 170-171; **Animals Animals:** 172-173; **Dave Starrett:** 178-179; **Ian Crysler:** 183;
Horizon: 187; **Ian Crysler:** 188-189, 191; **Dave Starrett:** 192-193; **Ian Crysler:** 198-199; **Dave Starrett:**
214, 218-219; **Everett Studios:** 224-225; **Richard Hutchings:** 226, 230; **Berenholtz/The Stock Market:**
233 TL; **Nick Nicholson/The Image Bank:** 233 BL; **Dennis Stock/Magnum Photos:** 233 TR; **Marcia Keegan/
The Stock Market:** 233 BR; © **Camerique/H. Armstrong Roberts:** 234 TR; **Michael Groen:** 234 BL, 235;
Everett Studios: 238-239; **Michael Groen:** 244-245; **Ian Crysler:** 251; **Ken Karp:** 252, 255; **Michael Groen:**
257; **Ken Karp:** 258, 259; **Michael Groen:** 260-261; **Dave Starrett:** 266-267; **Ian Crysler:** 272; © **Grant
Black/ First Light Toronto:** 277 T; © **Yvette Cardozo/Tony Stone Images:** 277 B; **Dave Starrett:** 278-279